Presenting Across Cultures

*How to adapt your business and sales
presentations in key markets around the world*

Ruben A. Hernandez

Presenting Across Cultures

Copyright © 2013 by Ruben A. Hernandez

ISBN 978-3-9815382-0-5

To my children

Contents

PART THREE

Acknowledgements

This book is the result of observations and interviews of people too numerous to name. Nevertheless, I would very much like to thank the nearly 130 people who allowed me to interview them formally for this project over the course of 7 years. They sat down with me on the telephone, on Skype, while attending my presentation seminars, in cafés, and at conferences, and graciously spent more time with me than the 30 minutes I assured them the interview would not exceed. I would also like to thank the nearly 700 international participants (non-German) who have attended my seminars from over 74 countries. They let me watch, question, push and probe them in my attempt to see where their personal and cultural boundaries were with regard to listening to and making a presentation.

Special mention and thanks goes to Daniel Thomas Halford and Bridget Gevaux for their editing skills and comments in helping me move this book forward to publication.

Preface

Quite honestly, the idea for this book was an after thought, given to me by a European publishing house when I approached them about another topic dear to me: an effective method for teaching presentation skills. The publishing house was interested in my proposal, but a week later they came to me with a special request. To distinguish the title from other "how to" books in this area they would also want a few chapters on presenting to different cultures.

Even though various workshops on intercultural communication are part of my training portfolio, I had never considered combining "presentations" and "culture" into a single topic. But not wanting to let the chance of publishing my method slip away, I shook my head yes and assured the editor that I could come up with something, that there was probably lots of material "out there" (somewhere) and it would only be just a question of finding it.

As I pursued my search for materials, it soon became evident that, in fact, very little was out there under the theme of cross-cultural presentations. Becoming somewhat anxious about this discovery, I decided to get a hold of some experts in the intercultural field from the Netherlands and the United States to see if they could steer me to some useful resources. The answer was always the same: *no one had yet looked at cross-cultural communication styles within the narrow confines of presentations in any depth.* They encouraged me to pursue this line of research and wished me luck. At that point, it became obvious that I would need more time for this project than originally planned. Indeed, unable to produce any significant volume of pages after a year – we parted company, amicably.

A number of years later, a book has finally materialized that focuses exclusively on making business presentations in other cultures, with specific recommendations on how to adapt to the desired structure, delivery style, "logical" arguments, listening patterns and visual support preferences of a given culture. My original idea about a methodology for teaching presentations was subsequently dropped as I became absorbed in researching a previously unexplored and, at least to me, an exciting area of cross-cultural communication. It has taken nearly 130 interviews with internationally-active business people and other trainers, as well as observing over 700 hundred international participants on my presentation seminars, not counting the locals (e.g. Germans).

What the book isn't, is an extensive guide on the *do's and don'ts* of surviving in the cultures examined herein. In large part because there are already many excellent titles on the market that can help the reader gain real insight and practical tips into doing business in different cultures. Some of those titles are listed in the bibliography. Rather, as the title suggests, the scope of this book concerns itself very narrowly with making presentations in over 20 different cultures and regions around the world. It is addressed primarily to an international business audience, but I am also confident that non business-related speakers will be able to glean useful information here.

You may notice, and perhaps ask why, some important markets did not make into the book (e.g. Turkey, Poland, Spain, Argentina, Chile, Indonesia, Thailand, the Philippines, and that swath of disparate cultures known as Sub-Saharan Africa). The reason for this is that either I did not have a sufficient number of their nationals on my seminars to observe them in action, or I was unable to find enough interview partners with enough insight to comment on their presentations styles. Often it was a combination of both. Hopefully, a future second edition can be offered which includes additional chapters of some of the cultures missing in this book this time.

Ruben A. Hernandez
Berg, Germany

Introduction

Doing business internationally will require you, at some point, to make business or sales presentations to a foreign audience. The size of that audience may vary, but the way a specific cultural group has learned to listen to information tends to conform to listening expectations about what's considered ideal – or even comprehensible.

There are numerous books and articles available today that focus on how to make an effective "international" presentation. They usually focus on how to make an effective presentation in a generic sense, e.g. "know your audience", "the tell them approach" (tell them what you'll say, say it, tell them what you said), or suggestions to "begin and end dynamically", "be clear and get straight to the point", "make it relevant to them", "practice your presentation" and so on. Much of this advice, however, has a strong Anglo-American flavor to it and no doubt would be quite useful in the English-speaking world.

But what about other cultural groups like the Japanese, Germans, or Italians to name a few? What exactly do people from these cultures consider to be clear, persuasive or even relevant information? What would, for example, *getting straight to the point* mean to them? In Japan, a good *first* presentation would include something about the speaker's relationship to Japan, no matter how tenuous it is. You would also need to say something about your company, your department, and then, after 20 minutes, begin looking at the systemic relationships that make up the background situation of your topic. To overlook these key connections would be

7

to miss the point completely from a Japanese perspective. In Germany, getting to the point may require moving straight to an in-depth analysis of what a product or technical solution does and *how it works* (anything less than "in depth" with lots of information is considered superficial). While in Italy, there's almost no bona fide point to a presentation at all. It is simply not the preferred venue of informing a group about business matters of any substance. Presentations, when given, are often seen as a mere perfunctory exercise – a type of cold appetizer before an interactive, candid discussion can begin.

So, *getting to the point* with an international audience requires, first, that we understand what *the point* is that we should be getting to. It requires the knowledge and ability to adapt to their listening expectations which, as this book will point out, differ from culture to culture.

These expectations tend to follow, but are not restricted to, various cultural dimensions which I've linked to communication patterns in presentations. Some of these dimensions will be familiar to those readers acquainted with intercultural terminology. Other dimensions have been specifically formulated to express values regularly touched upon in presentations.

In total, the profiles offered in this book look at how 16 different cultural groups ideally prefer to hear, see and experience a business presentation. There is also a section on what to do if you present in front of an internationally mixed audience. Specific recommendations are given that will help you adapt your structure, style, opening, logical development, summary, and language to each audience. Insights are also included to help you construct a persuasive argument and appealing message from culture to culture.

Readers will need to consider, however, that we are looking at cultural tendencies which necessitate speaking in generalities. Of course, an individual's unique personality and experience can supersede the cultural profiles described in this book. Audiences will also differ within a given culture – depending on their special areas of expertise or interest. That's why it's important to distinguish between what an individual might do actively when giving a presentation and what that same individual will understand, filtered through cultural reference points, when listening to one. We will be looking at those shared cultural reference points which make *listening* to a presentation comprehensible on a broad level within a culture.

The outline of each profile

Each country-specific article contains three sections totaling, on average, 2,200 words. In the first section, you will get a **profile graph** using 13 cultural dimensions, each along a values continuum pertaining to presentations. The dimensions are discussed in the first chapter entitled: **Cultural Dimensions and Presentations**. A distribution curve is placed along each continuum to provide, at a glance, the relative position and importance a culture places on a given value. In the second section, you will receive a 2-3 page exposé that is further subdivided into two parts. Part one, **First Things First**, offers some basic information on general attitudes and behavior of the selected country that you should consider before even giving a presentation there. The second, and much lengthier part, is sub-headed: **The Presentation**. It covers speaker attributes, the opening structure and things to consider in the content and persuasion points, the summary, and the Q&A format. The recommendations are oriented toward business presentations, but non-business speakers will also glean useful information here. Finally, in section three, you will get a list of **likes and dislikes** (dos and don'ts) as a bullet-point summary of each exposé.

PART ONE

Cultural Dimensions and Business Presentations

1

Interpreting the
Presentation Profile Graph

Intercultural training workshops have become a standard offering in almost all internationally active companies today. For those who have attended them, one way they have learned to look at culture is through contrasting values along a continuum, commonly known as cultural dimensions. These are typically used by intercultural experts and academics to describe cultures in broader terms. Some of these dimensions, however, corresponded nicely at a narrower level when used to characterize different aspects of international presentations. In other cases (i.e. dimensions 2, 3, 4, 7, 8 and 12), I have submitted new dimensions that are merely descriptive, based on speaker preferences in business, technical and sales presentations.

While reading, keep in mind that culture influences what we look at and what we consider important information. But in every culture there will always be a distribution of preferences for what is considered important. The question is to determine where, between each set of values, the hump occurs, and what it means with regard to adapting our presentations.

A simple key to interpreting the profile graph in each chapter is the following:

1. The curve is equally distributed in the two segments. This suggests both values are important and should be integrated in the presentation (i.e. spend equal time on problem and solution).

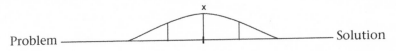

2. The curve falls more to one segment. This suggests that you should stress the more dominant value but not completely neglect the minor one (e.g. on the product-market continuum, time would be spent talking about the product, but most of your time would be devoted to analyzing the market for it).

3. The curve is situated mostly on one side with three quarters of it in one segment. This suggests a strong emphasis on a given value with little or no need to integrate the minor value into your presentation (e.g. maintain a formal, professional demeanor with the audience and avoid chumminess altogether).

1. Task vs. Relationship orientation considers to what degree a relationship is first required before even making a presentation. Task-oriented cultures tend to be deal-focused and can often do business with strangers – with relatively little interpersonal exchange. Relationship cultures, on the other hand, need to know who they are working with before doing business. This is critical. Even the chance to make a presentation is usually the result of first establishing a relationship with an important intermediary. At the level of a presentation in a relationship-oriented culture, a speaker will also need to provide a more detailed introduction of himself, his company, and any previous contact the speaker has had with the host company and country. It is not uncommon for the introduction to be the longest segment of a presentation in some relationship-oriented cultures. In most task-oriented cultures, the presentation would be finished in that time.

2. Extensive background vs. limited background context is an aspect of the task vs. relationship dimension. It looks at how extensively the speaker should explain the background context implicit in any presentation. There is a fairly strong correlation between the degree to which a culture is relationship-oriented and the extent the interconnecting *relationships* that make up the background of any presentation need to be made explicit to the audience. The causal links need to be intricately woven into a rich contextual picture before there can be any talk of products, solutions, proposals or new strategies. Without it, a presentation will appear rushed and incomplete. Even if the speaker thinks the audience already knows the situation, it is still a good idea to present the background. In many cases, the audience wants to be convinced that the speaker understands the situation as well. Those cultures that require limited background usually want just enough to "put them in the picture" (maybe as little as a one-line reference) or no background at all, just beginning by stating the purpose of the presentation.

3. Problem analysis vs. solution focus explores where the focus of the presentation should be when proposing a new idea or solution to a problem. It may strike some as self-evident that any presentation articulating a solution should focus on just that, but there are cultures that view solutions and proposals as sequentially dependent on whether one truly grasps the situation first. In other words, in their view, understanding the situation will suggest an answer. The solution is almost anti-climactic. A speaker should then invest time and finesse in explaining how the different areas impacting on a problem are linked. Otherwise, what you are proposing will be viewed as premature and could end up being costly for everyone involved. For other cultures, the stress should be on a solution analysis. They prefer to hear only a cursory explanation of the problem, backed by hard data, with more focus on the solution – or, ideally, on a number of solutions.

4. Product focus vs. market focus looks at where the emphasis should be when introducing a new product or service. Some cultural groups think that if a product is terrific, a market will naturally arise. Its inherent usefulness, quality, or beauty is the drawing factor, and people will see its value on their own once they understand the features of the product. A lot of other cultural groups think that there are many great ideas and products on the market, but if you don't market them correctly, if the logistic base isn't there to distribute them, if the features are not presented in a compelling way, then the product will not succeed. They believe you need to convince people that great ideas are great. Often it is only a question of emphasis, but it is exactly where you put the emphasis that will make a product, service, or idea resonate with a specific culture, or not.

5. Individual vs. Group identity is a dimension that looks at who to focus on when framing the benefits of something: as a benefit to the individual or to a group that shares strongly in a collective affiliation. In some cultures, you will need to point out the benefits to the group in order for them to be convinced of its intrinsic value. The goals of the group are as important as, and sometimes even trump, the goals of the individual. For other cultures, individual identity and behavior are defined separately from the group. The stress here needs to be on the benefits for the individual, especially in achieving advancement or self-expression. A well-known example of this was the Sony Walkman. In the East, it allowed one to listen to music without disturbing others. In the West, it provided the listener with high-quality listening pleasure and allowed for the individual freedom to go anywhere, and listen to anything at any time.

6. High-context vs. Low-context communication (Indirect vs. Direct communication) looks at how much meaning is found in the context of a communication exchange versus how much is found in the explicit words themselves. High context cultures are aware of the verbal and nonverbal cues that help determine meaning. In particular, information that may be interpreted as unfavorable will often be expressed indirectly so that no one loses face. Someone who is too direct or "tactless" is considered rude with little regard for relationships or other people's feelings. Someone from a high-context culture is usually quite skilled at expressing negative information indirectly. By the same token, listeners in these cultures typically have well-developed antenna to pick up signals (e.g. body language, changes in the voice, critical information that is left out, etc.) that help them comprehend the intended message. Cultures that are low-context place more meaning in the spoken language itself. Here, communication tends to be specific, explicit and direct. Opinions can be openly given because it is generally assumed by the listener, in low-context cultures, that the intent of the person voicing an opinion is not to hurt someone's feelings, but to be clear and authentic. This dimension is important when considering how to communicate negative information around the world.

7. Engaging vs. Neutral delivery (includes body language) points out the degree to which cultures link body language, gestures, and voice to credibility. In some cultures, if a speaker is too engaging, too charismatic, or too enthusiastic, then audiences will perceive this as the speaker hiding something behind what they see as *contrived* energy. It is viewed as an attempt to distract from the truth. Other cultures reach a similar conclusion with the opposite level of expressiveness. They believe that if a speaker is too neutral and too subdued, then it must mean that the speaker himself is not convinced of his own words. The lack of passion gives away the speaker's lack of interest and belief: "it's just a job; I need the paycheck".

8. Figurative vs. Rational expressions takes into account how to make an idea "clear" to the audience. Some cultures require examples, analogies, metaphors and anecdotes. They quite literally need to visualize the speaker's idea. Other cultures perceive the use of many examples and analogies as speaking down to them, as questioning their intelligence. Rather, they expect complex ideas to be explained through sharp analysis and precise, rational concepts. Examples and metaphors will sometimes be used in cultures that favor rational expressions, but they will be kept to maybe one or two in a 20-30 minute presentation.

9. Deductive vs. Inductive thinking looks at the reasoning process used to arrive at an assertion. Broadly speaking, some cultures prefer that you discuss a general proposition first and then link it to specific applications or real-life situations (in that order). They begin with a theory or assumption and then speak at length before following up with an example. With other cultures, the reverse is true. They would want a speaker to note numerous reality-based examples of a situation, and then follow with a concluding principle that links the multiple examples given to a general premise. It is important to keep in mind here, however, that no culture would consider either of the two irrelevant. Both are indispensable when substantiating a claim. It is simply a question of where the starting point is and how much emphasis is given to each.

10. Risk averse vs. Risk inclined examines the relationship between risk and the amount of information perceived to be necessary in a presentation. Risk-averse cultures will often require lots of information, details, facts and carefully thought-through propositions, with all the possible downsides thoroughly investigated. Communication must be explicit and extensive, with nothing left to chance and nothing left for the audience to assume for themselves. More risk-inclined cultures, on the other hand, prefer a general picture of the situation and the general steps that will lead to success. They develop a "feel" for the potential success of an idea through first understanding the big picture. If the big picture is clear and attractive, then they will enquire further. Risk-inclined cultures tend to dislike overly detailed presentations and grow restless if too much is being presented too soon.

11. Formal vs. Informal (hierarchy vs. equality) is linked to the unwritten rules of personal interaction in a society. It looks at the degree of formality or familiarity one has with others – especially with those that are not part of one's inner circle. The dimension generally reflects a society's attitude toward hierarchy or equality. With regard to presentations, formality will manifest in a number of ways. A speaker, for example, will be expected to maintain the use of titles (e.g. Mr, Mrs, Dr, Professor) and honorific names (e.g. Sheikh, Sama) when referring to oneself and others. To drop them when required will create a feeling of awkwardness among those wishing to address the speaker. Formality will also reflect in the way one dresses for a presentation and the professional demeanor to be kept. For example, a presenter should avoid trying to be chummy or too congenial with the audience, otherwise risk losing respect. On the other hand, in more equality-oriented societies, keeping too great a distance, other than what is considered professional behavior, can be interpreted as arrogance – provoking the audience to find a way to bring the speaker "down" to their level. That is why first names are often used; it is a serious attempt to appear modest and approachable.

12. Use of humor vs. Seriousness is an extension of the formal vs. informal dimension which, nevertheless, requires its own grouping. It is perhaps the one dimension of presentations most frequently asked about by seminar participants. Either of these poles can go a long way to winning or losing audience support for a speaker. Of course, when using humor, it is important first to distinguish between the different kinds of humor that might be acceptable to some audiences (e.g. wit, a funny story or example, self-deprecating humor, etc.) and certain types that should be avoided altogether (e.g. sarcasm and puns, which are often misunderstood in an international setting anyway, and off-color jokes). For some cultures, a funny story is a welcome method for energizing the audience. In informal, equality-oriented cultures, self-deprecating humor is a reliable antidote against pretentiousness, or "taking oneself too seriously", which would be a damaging perception to convey. On the other hand, others cultures will perceive almost any kind of humor during a presentation as inappropriate. It would be viewed as flippant, unserious or, even worse, not funny.

The energy will then turn to a feeling of awkwardness and embarrassment among the listeners, and respect for the speaker will take a nosedive.

13. Time fixed vs. Time fluid highlights a culture's approach to time. With time-fixed (or time-precise) cultures, time takes on a material quality. It can be given, saved, wasted, spent, won, lost and, very importantly, finely divided. Time is a valuable commodity to be scheduled tightly, quite often to maximize the number of activities one can do in a day, year or lifetime. When giving a presentation, the time needed for it is usually articulated at the start (or written in an agenda and distributed beforehand). The audience needs to know how much time it will take, and they will tend to become anxious if the time needed runs over the allotted period. If there are actions to be carried out by the listeners from time-fixed cultures, then it is understood by everyone that those actions are expected to be completed on time. For cultures that are time-fluid, typically more relationship and consensus-oriented cultures, time is more abstract and intangible. It does not lead but follows the contours of life. For a presentation, stating its duration beforehand would be unusual. Those from time-fluid cultures would find it puzzling if the speaker rushed through an important part of a talk just to meet some artificial time constraint. Timelines for projects can and are given, but it is generally understood by everyone that they are only approximations; much flexibility is built in. The unpredictable demands of personal and professional relationships will upset the best laid plans. Add to that unforeseen occurrences, like technical mishaps, accidents, undependable suppliers, and bad weather and the idea that actions can be planned precisely, is an absurd notion at best.

PART TWO

Making Business and
Sales Presentations:
Country Profiles

2

Making Presentations
in the Arab World

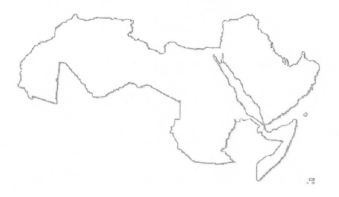

I. Presentation Profile –
The Arab World

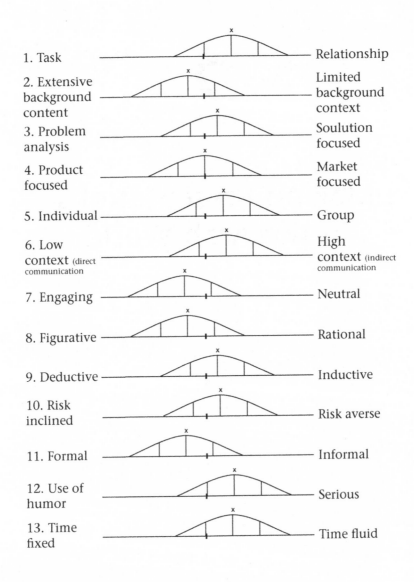

1. Task — Relationship
2. Extensive background content — Limited background context
3. Problem analysis — Soulution focused
4. Product focused — Market focused
5. Individual — Group
6. Low context (direct communication — High context (indirect communication
7. Engaging — Neutral
8. Figurative — Rational
9. Deductive — Inductive
10. Risk inclined — Risk averse
11. Formal — Informal
12. Use of humor — Serious
13. Time fixed — Time fluid

II. Exposé –
Making Presentations in the Arab World
(North Africa and the Arab Gulf States)

First things first

(For the purpose of this exposé, the Arab world, or Arabs, will refer to those countries where Arabic is the sole official language, with the exception of Iraq).

It is very important to develop relationships in the Arab world, as it is the key factor in driving business. Indeed, perhaps the only country that rivals in importance for business outside this region is Japan. Keep in mind, however, that a general practice in the Arab world is to work through a local partner. You could begin by going to the local chamber of commerce or one representing that country in your homeland and asking who would be an appropriate agent. The agent will help guide you through the fine points of doing business in the country you're visiting.

You should allow for an introductory period (sometimes a week) to initiate relationship-building. This will include informal conversations, small talk about each other's family (though enquiring about a man's wife is considered unacceptable), work and culture. Resist talking about business until your host makes the first move.

Sending a young, low-level representative from your company will not make a good impression from your side – unless he's meeting with an equally low-level delegate. The more senior level person your agent arranges for you to meet, the more senior must be the representative from your company as well. Anyone lower in rank is a sign of disrespect.

In most of the Arab world, and particularly in the Gulf States, religion (Islam) pervades daily life to a degree unknown in most other countries. References to Allah or the Prophet Mohammed are intertwined in personal and business discussions. Should you enter into a religious discussion you should avoid saying you are an atheist, even if you are. Such a statement is considered primitive in the Islamic world, on par with saying you can't read or don't wash yourself. It is enough to mention the religious milieu you grew up in and avoid any form of religious debate altogether. You might also consider arranging your schedule around Ramadan – as you should not openly eat, drink or smoke during the daylight hours at this time. On Fridays, businesses are closed.

When your chance to make a presentation arrives, it will most likely be to lower-level technical experts or managers. They, in turn, will inform the highest-level managers or boss – all of whom depend on their support staff for advice. By no means should you attempt to go straight to the top – unless it is the "top" who is approaching you.

Having a woman lead your team can present difficulties. This is not because Arabs think women don't possess a keen sense of business acumen. They are fully aware that women can be just as competent as men in business and, in many areas, often better. Rather, this has much more to do with the need to form solid relationships. It would be personally compromising for an Arab businessman or manager to invite a woman (without her husband) home to his wife, mother-in-law and children; the practice of inviting home a business guest with whom a relationship is developing is quite common in the Middle East. In any event, this would put your Arab-male client in a difficult position, one he would probably just avoid by showing no interest in your product or service.

The presentation

The speaker

Arabs like good, creative speakers who are eloquent and can magically create powerful images in the mind of their listeners. However, reading from a script or PowerPoint slides, or coming across as too low-key, dry and rational may result in your completely disappearing from their radar screens. In a region of the world where intense sounds, smells and tastes exist around every corner, it is to be expected that individual personalities will need to *make their mark* to get noticed by a group. It is no less a challenge with a presentation, where a speaker must demonstrate his skill with charm, flattery, story-telling, erudition, competency, conviction and emotion. You will also need to make good eye-contact to show you are a sincere speaker. (Even with the best speakers, however, there is never a guarantee that the entire audience will give you its undivided attention. You may find some members carrying on their own conversation in spite of your best efforts. If this is the case, it is best to just continue and take no notice.)

The above description, especially of a charismatic speaker, does not mean that one should be loud. A speaker should be clearly audible, but keep in mind that there are volume swings in Arabic unlike very few other languages. Indeed, typically when a very important point is being made in Arabic, the tempo and volume come down considerably, where the words are expressed in a noticeably soft-spoken but well-enunciated manner. The sound of your voice and how you use the language (even your own) are just as important as the content. The "sound" must be agreeable to the ear.

The speaker himself must be very competent. A strong academic title will help. But Arabs also need to be reassured that you are competent. Their antennas are fine-tuned to hear who really is competent and who is merely trying to give that impression without the know-how behind it.

Before beginning with your topic, you should mention how nicely you've been received, the generosity of the hosts and something interesting you've seen in the country. Arabs love eloquence and colorful metaphors, both of which play an important role in the language. And there is no better way to weave these two together than in a flattering remark. *"Thank you for your selfless generosity, Mr Habib. Even your smallest gesture possesses the striking brilliance of a polished diamond.* In the end, remember to bring honor and recognition to your hosts and to avoid using your presentation as a venue for any kind of self-promotion.

The opening structure

Your presentation should be well-structured but not overly so. It should give the audience a sense of where they're going and how they will get there. But they want to see your personality come through in a free-speaking format. There should be a "talking to the audience" quality to it, as if you are recounting a story. In other words, you should not present stiffly, referring to notes (in your hands or projected on a screen). If you outline your presentation in a way that lists more than five points – with additional sub-points – then it will probably turn off your audience right from the start. They will see that there's much too much information in it for their liking. You can make your handouts very detailed, but not your talk.

Arabs are quite high-context in their communication style. Therefore, they will need (and like) for you at the beginning to set the scene for your talk by painting a rather extensive background context. They need to see the bigger picture here. They will then attempt to relate the rest of your talk to that context in order to make sense of your message. So take your time and construct it well.

Content and points of persuasion

If you are presenting a product or service, it is best to focus on the country you're in. Arabs are only minimally interested in how the product or service works in another (including Arab) country. What they especially want to know is how it can be applied to their situation. Unless they ask specifically, it is enough to say that your product *"in other areas in the region has worked quite well"* – if, and only if, that is indeed the case. More importantly, you will need to demonstrate how those listening will gain in some way, either personally or for their company, in prestige or in profits (you should not underestimate the value of prestige in the Arab world).

As already hinted above, the effective power of a talk can be more compelling to Arab audiences than a purely linear, rational argumentation approach. This does not mean, however, that you can bluff your way through a presentation by only trying to rouse emotions, which would be a serious error. Your audience will take it for granted that your product or service is of a given quality, especially if you are representing a reputable company. You will need to point out its advantages for their specific context, but do it in a way that is "convincing", which loops back to "how" you present your point of view.

Keep in mind that exaggeration and embellishment are not seen in a negative light by most Arab audiences. Indeed, they are interpreted as signals which indicate to the audience, "this is important". It is a form of bringing light (attention) to that which needs to be seen and might otherwise be missed.

It might be prudent to avoid giving overly technical, abstract and theoretical explanations in your presentations. It is not that your Arab audience can't handle it, but it is often perceived as pedantic. A common critique Arabs have of Westerners is that they *"come in as the experts who need to show us what is good for us"*, or *"They think they need to teach us – as though they always know better about what we need than we ourselves"*. It can be fatal if you are perceived as trying to be "the teacher". They turn off quickly – and may even make a comment that expresses their discontent. Therefore, it is probably best to be careful how you phrase your recommendations by padding your suggestions with expressions such as, *"You would perhaps like to know that this feature could be useful"*. *"There is option A and option B – and selecting the right one will depend on what you think is important for your situation."*

It is best to be honest *and* enthusiastic in your presentation delivery style. Arabs love enthusiasm *and* emotion. They also admire those who consciously take a position – and are suspicious of those who think they are only being objective. In the Arab world, they are aware that so-called objective facts exist. And yet, individuals are always subjective in the way they select "facts". They believe that you should never deceive yourself into thinking that you're being truly "objective". They think it is simply better to admit to yourself that you do, in fact, hold a subjective position and be emotionally honest about it. That's why they look for emotion as an indicator of genuine belief and honesty, and because they do not believe that one should disengage oneself from his message. For many Northern Europeans, and particularly Asians, expressing enthusiasm or profound conviction is not always easy. There is an acceptable alternative, however. Arab audiences are used to hearing stories and anecdotes within a presentation. Here, one might learn to develop a poignant story that will touch them emotionally. Do not be afraid to go off on these digressions; the audience is used to it. They will not only be able to follow, but they'll also remember exactly that point where you diverged and easily pick up the strand again.

In a manner similar to Asia, communicating criticism or bad news in the Arab world cannot be done directly. To do so can have a devastating effect on your relationship – and on the way you (and your company) will be perceived in the future. It is best to avoid attributing blame (taken as shame in the Arab world) to a specific person or group. It is better to simply point out the problem tactfully and then move on to the desired result. For example, if you need to present the disappointing results of a clinical trial for a new drug to the team of pharmaceutical experts that developed it, it would be best simply to say, *"We will need more time to develop this product"*. Your intended meaning will be clear to everyone involved, in large part because Arab listeners will cooperate with the speaker to understand the general idea rather than focus only on specific content.

Likewise, Arabs do not mind hearing your product compared to your competitors, but it is enough to simply say "our competitors". You do not need to name names or put others in a bad light.

A presentation should avoid discussing something to death. Your audience does not want to be saturated with endless facts and details (as is often the case in Germany, France and Russia). Too much scrutiny will drive them to impatience. When you do present details, it should always lead to making the big picture more complete, more understandable. Your main points, however, should be repeated numerous times and in different ways throughout the presentation (e.g. sometimes using examples, analogies and metaphors) to get your point across. This is a commonly used method among Arabic speakers themselves.

Time is fluid in the Arab world. Mid to long-term planning can be given, but it is understood by everyone that they are only approximations; a great deal of flexibility should be included in any milestone timetable. To assume that long-term plans should take place as scheduled borders on arrogance in the Arab world. For man can never presume to know the future. It is a domain that belongs exclusively to God. To demonstrate time flexibility in your presentation is not a sign of pessimism. Rather, to Arabs, it is a sign of prudence and a realistic attitude towards life.

Those doing business in the Arab world need to distinguish between state-owned businesses and privately-held ones. This is particularly true in the North African countries of Egypt, Libya, Algeria and Morocco. State-owned businesses will tend to make decisions in large part on price, existing relationships and questionable incentives. If they perceive your profit margin is too high or if your sales representative is *too* stylishly dressed (North African bureaucrats will equate over-dressed reps with over-priced products), then your chances of succeeding could be significantly reduced. The privately-held companies in North Africa will want a fair price, but more importantly, they will want to know if they can make a profit.

The Arab Gulf States, on the other hand, are richer and more status-conscious. Depending on where you find yourself in the Gulf, and in which industry, there is a good chance that you will be working with a foreign expatriate. If this is the case, then you will have to adapt your approach and dress accordingly. The final word on major decisions, however, will be made by a national of that country (a local Sheikh or other high-ranking person). Getting the cheapest price is rarely a consideration in the Gulf. Rather, knowing they have the best product or service, especially from a company that has a good world-wide reputation, is very important. Quality and status is the perfect combination in the Gulf region.

The summary

Your summary should be concise and a true distillation of what your key message is. It should not, however, be the first time they have heard your key message. It should be given repeatedly, in different ways, throughout the presentation. When something is truly important, Arabs will emphasize this by constantly repeating it.

Q&A

Questions in the Arab world come in two phases: at the end, and after the officially designated Q&A period. You will need to remain to take questions that members of your audience prefer to ask face to face.

Final points

If you are going to use slides, pictures etc., do not use pictures which could be embarrassing to your audience. For example, it may be romantic for a Westerner to show a local farmer riding a donkey or desert nomads and their camels. But this would only be interpreted negatively in the Arab world as if you are trying to point out either their poverty or lack of modernity. Handouts should be given during or after the presentation – and not before-hand.

Dress conservatively and professionally. In the Gulf States, you may need to upgrade a bit. What you wear should reflect your status within your company as well as the status of the people you will be dealing with. Appearance is important.

III. Dos and Don'ts

With regard to presentations Arabs need or like:
- Respect and honor for your hosts
- Charisma, flattery, emotion and eloquence
- The ability to be soft-spoken
- Competence in topic area
- A speaker's personal opinion
- Structure, but not too much detail
- A richly-woven background context
- Examples and colorful analogies
- Product or service applications specific to their situation
- Knowledge of how they will gain in prestige or profit
- Flexibility with plans, schedules, and milestones
- Repetition of key points, often and in different ways
- Opportunities to ask questions after the official Q&A session

...and they don't need or like:

- A speaker who reads his presentation (i.e. PowerPoint text)
- Someone who comes across as if they're trying to teach them
- Direct criticism
- Disrespect for the hierarchy, e.g. if you try to go straight to the top

3

Making Presentations
in Brazil

IV. Presentation Profile - Brazil

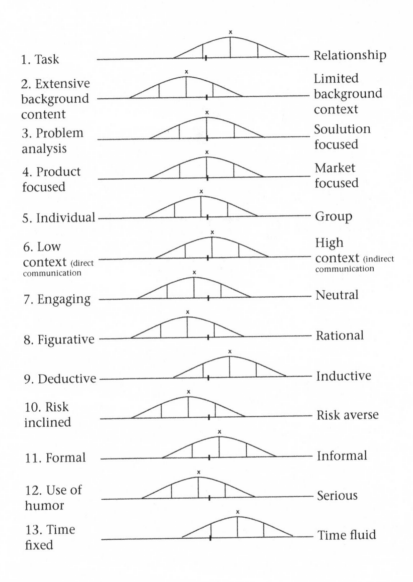

1. Task — Relationship

2. Extensive background content — Limited background context

3. Problem analysis — Soulution focused

4. Product focused — Market focused

5. Individual — Group

6. Low context (direct communication — High context (indirect communication

7. Engaging — Neutral

8. Figurative — Rational

9. Deductive — Inductive

10. Risk inclined — Risk averse

11. Formal — Informal

12. Use of humor — Serious

13. Time fixed — Time fluid

II. Exposé –
Making Presentations in Brazil

First things first

Brazil is most definitely a relationship-oriented society. They need to know who (company and representative) they are doing business with – *in person and in some depth* – before they can even consider doing business with you. One cannot simply arrive and expect to make a presentation having had only minimal contact – unless you have been invited to make an *academic* presentation at a conference. In the business world, you should be aware that the moment you appear to the moment you leave is all part of your presentation.

Brazilians are warm and demonstrative, and they feel comfortable with others who can show their emotion and enthusiasm for life as well. That said, they are aware that even though *"Deus é brasileiro" (God is Brazilian)*, other cultures have other temperaments. They expect Germans and Scandinavians, for example, to be a bit drier and reserved and will become suspicious if someone is trying to be more Brazilian than they. Of course, they will be pleasantly delighted if you can show some *genuine* emotion, warmth and "humanity", without overdoing it. Showing "humanity" means seeing that a foreign business partner does not live to work but rather works to live. Specifically, this means that you can talk about your family, that you're empathetic, that you like Brazil and that you are interested in your Brazilian hosts as people, regardless of what they can do for your business. They are cautious of those who only see "dollars" – thinking they will sacrifice any relationship for the sake of money. Therefore, establishing a solid relationship will be the key to gaining their trust.

The Presentation

The speaker

Brazilians can be quite charismatic speakers, bordering on the theatrical. They are able to speak freely yet coherently in a way few can match in the whole of Latin America (with the exception of Cuba). A speaker should look like they enjoy being with the audience and talking about their chosen topic. He should be friendly, compassionate and optimistic. Unlike presenters in many Spanish-speaking Latin-American countries, Brazilians expect a speaker to be competent in his topic but not authoritative in his attitude. One should be "simpático" (nice, pleasant) and, of course, friendly. This reflects a strong egalitarian ethos found in Brazil (and especially São Paolo) among the educated and professional classes. A speaker is free to give his opinion on anything, but there should be no trace of absoluteness in that view.

A good sense of humor is very important, and having self-deprecating humor is perceived as one of the key attributes to being seen in a favorable light. Of course, in serious situations, humor should be avoided.

Flexibility is perhaps the most universally admired quality of Brazilians. If, when presenting, you are able to bring this quality across (e.g. offer various options for a solution, be able to change your original plan, build some flexibility into your presentation structure, or even respond flexibly to some unforeseen situation like the projector breaking down) you will be seen very favorably. Remember, the presentation is more than your "talk" to an audience.

Opening structure

Business presentations should be structured, though structure should not dominate. It should be embedded in the talk so as to

40

give a feeling that there is some organization to it. Most of all, there should be a sense that you are talking directly to your audience. If you are a speaker who likes to present an outline, then only include 3-5 key points. Avoid dividing up the talk into sub points or sub-sub points. This will dishearten your audience and lead to a perceived stiffness, which they hope you'll avoid.

Begin with some words about yourself and your company. Gauge the time that you will dedicate to this compared to the overall length of your talk. If you have a generous amount of time, then take some it to talk a little more about your company. If time is limited, then keep it correspondingly short. But what you cannot do is simply jump right into the topic. They want to know something about you and who you're representing. Again, based on the amount of time you have, you might also include a few very favorable impressions you have of Brazil.

Brazilians require a rather extensive background context at the beginning of the presentation. All important and related factors should be presented. You will need to weave a picture that they can visualize and use as a setting for all subsequent parts of the presentation.

Content and points of persuasion

With product/service presentations, you will be expected to also discuss the needs or problems your product or service can resolve. These needs should be genuine, however; they cannot be contrived or perceived as superficial. In this way, the problem discussion is a type of buildup to your benefits. As a non-Brazilian, you will have to show how these problems are also relevant in Brazil. You will also gain much credibility if you can demonstrate that you've listened to and involved Brazilians in the solution. Otherwise you will sound like you're there to prescribe an answer from the "outside" – a perception that will seriously hurt your chances of getting anything accepted.

In some countries, out-of-the-box thinking can be viewed with skepticism. In Brazil, however, the more creative your solution is, the more attractive it will be perceived. Therefore, do not be shy about stressing a product's uniqueness or its newness – especially some creative aspect of it. In general, creativity is an important quality that Brazilians admire, so you will win points by distinguishing yourself here.

Product presentations do not have to be purely rational in Brazil, with a "stick-only-to-the-features" delivery. You can also introduce personal anecdotes in your presentation (e.g. how even your young children were able to use the software without Dad having to read the user manual). This approach will also make you sound more human in the eyes of your Brazilian audience – a definite plus.

On the other hand, as much as Brazilians like clever and creatively designed products, they have a strong pragmatic bent when it comes to business. You may have a great product, but if there is no perceived market, Brazilians will be hesitant about trying to create one for it. Here you will need to do your homework and find out what they really need, or stress a certain aspect of your product in order to awaken their interest. Doing this research is actually easier than it might appear, and having Brazilian partners will be an asset here.

Brazilians are, on the whole, quite risk-friendly. Part of this is due to their history in the 60s, 70s, and 80s of not knowing what new policy their constantly changing government would implement. As a result, they learned to act quickly and decisively on sparse information. If they have a "feeling" that something is right, they act on it. You do not need to go on and on with endless arguments.

Brazilian listening patterns tend to be proactively dynamic. This is a technical way of saying that they finish ideas for you (while listening to you), often interpreting your message before they have even finished listening to it. The conflation of ideas between speaker and listener can often lead to an unintended meaning. To avoid this, you will need to repeat your main message explicitly, at least a few times. Provide concrete examples and anecdotes (or even diagrams) so that your listeners can hear and see your message in different ways. Also, pay attention to any questions raised by the audience during or after your talk. Listen for any hint of misunderstanding. Then, seek to clarify your point. And, of course, avoid ascribing blame with comments like, "*you misunderstood me, let me explain it to you again*".

For complex ideas, or purely rational and complicated explanations, it is best to use a creative example, metaphor or analogy to help with understanding. Like most relatively young cultures (e.g. Australia, Argentina, or the USA), Brazilians can be quite playful with their language, with analogies and metaphors that are typically part of their everyday communication pattern.

If you are an expert in your field, Brazilians will want to hear your recommendations for any action to be taken. They will expect you to have mapped out the precise steps leading to success.

As with most relationship cultures, you will need to be careful how you communicate negative information or criticism. Diplomacy and a humble tone should be employed. No one should lose face in front of the group. Of course, you should also avoid making any comments that would put Brazil in a bad light. This may seem self-evident, but there are numerous examples of foreign visitors for whom this was not obvious. For example, one Northern European visitor, upon arriving late for his presentation, started his talk by sharing the reason he was late. He told the audience that he was robbed by a ghetto gang. In such a distressing situation like that it is understandable that one should want to seek empathy. Nevertheless, keep in mind that any culture in the world would feel ashamed if that happened in their country to a guest. Brazilians are especially sensitive here, so announcing it would be an instant mood killer.

The summary

The summary is an important element in Brazilian presentations for two main reasons. First, a speaker should not waste this opportunity by simply repeating the general categories of what was spoken about – a kind of outline in the past tense (e.g. "we discussed the strategy we need to take to remain competitive"). This type of summary says nothing and would be a lost opportunity to repeat your key message one more time. Remember, Brazilians will often interpret for you, running the risk of conveying an unintended meaning. Secondly, the ending should be something that provokes thought and emotion (but not be pessimistic). To combine these two factors is considered the ultimate in Brazil, so it is a great way to end your talk there.

Q&A

You can expect your Brazilian audience to ask questions during and after the presentation. Do not feel that you have to rush through this for time's sake. Brazil is a very time-fluid culture and they will think you are unprofessional if you, for the sake of the clock, give incomplete answers to questions they perceive as important.

Final points

Dress professionally. Even with engineers you should dress smart-casual. Brazilians place great importance on how you dress. Whether you like it or not, they will assess you on this level as well.

III. Dos and Don'ts:

With regard to presentations, the **Brazilians** need or like:

- Charismatic speakers who enjoy speaking freely to the audience
- Friendly and optimistic speakers with warmth and a sense of humor
- Flexibility in the speaker and the presentation
- Some structure, but it shouldn't dominate
- Some information about the speaker's company and personal bio
- A well-developed background
- Creative solutions – but with their situation considered in the solution
- Personal anecdotes, metaphors and analogies
- Concrete examples
- Recommendations and precise steps from experts
- Repetition of important ideas
- Brazil shown in a good light
- Lively question and answer discussion

...and they don't need or like:

- Just the facts, a business-only attitude
- Direct criticism of anyone
- Prescribed solutions
- A rushed presentation or question and answer session
- Too casual dress

4

Making Presentations in China

I. Presentation Profile - China

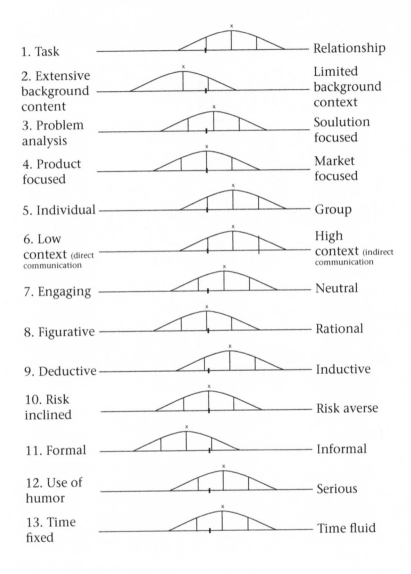

1. Task		Relationship
2. Extensive background content		Limited background context
3. Problem analysis		Soulution focused
4. Product focused		Market focused
5. Individual		Group
6. Low context (direct communication		High context (indirect communication
7. Engaging		Neutral
8. Figurative		Rational
9. Deductive		Inductive
10. Risk inclined		Risk averse
11. Formal		Informal
12. Use of humor		Serious
13. Time fixed		Time fluid

II. Exposé –
Making Presentations in China

First things first

The warm-up period in China is an important step in developing a personalized network of influence, known as "Guanxi". This is true not only in business but in Chinese society in general. It is not just the relationship with another individual that should be viewed here, but the connections you and your prospective partner bring to that relationship. Without it, very little can be accomplished – especially when it comes to favors. Whether given to you or requested from your side, know that they must always be repaid.

The very first step in relationship building in China is to show respect to everyone, especially those whom the Chinese themselves ascribe it to: the elderly or most senior members in a group, and those with titles. If you come from an egalitarian, achievement-oriented society, you may want to consider sending an older, more senior and academically-qualified colleague within your group to give the presentation as a sign of respect. To be an expert in the subject matter should be a secondary consideration here. Most foreigners start out at a deficit with the Chinese – as they have an inherent mistrust of them. It is something you will need to work hard at to overcome. So make sure your relationship-building skills are as good as any idea being proposed.

That said, you will still need to be as authentic as possible. The Chinese can easily spot someone who is not genuine. They especially esteem those who are poised, serene, relaxed, but serious. In the "getting-to-know-you" phase the Chinese are not so interested in seeing *what* you know, but rather *who* you are, namely, your character. In the West we tend to exchange information about ourselves. In the East, they want to get a "feel" for the person, and they are

49

constantly scanning to determine who they are dealing with. They admire those with good judgment, those who can listen (they'll be listening to see if you can listen), reflect and *filter* their conversation. They are able to learn about you by what you don't say as well. For example, if you talk about your wife but do not mention children, they will assume you don't have any. It is clear to them and they will not enquire further. Likewise, the Chinese (and, even more so, the Japanese) will expect you to be able to listen to them in this manner yourself – especially where the topic might cause one to lose face.

There are some topics you might want to avoid as they can cause conflict (e.g. their political system, industrial copyright infringements, air pollution, human rights, etc.) Unlike the Japanese or Thais, the Chinese can explode quite unexpectedly and be quite aggressive if they perceive their national pride or "face" is not respected. On the other hand, flattery is welcomed if given sincerely (or, at least, skillfully). Chances are, however, that you will have a translator in China who will fine-tune and filter your message if you stumble.

The Presentation

The Speaker and Introduction

As mentioned above, it is important to show respect to your Chinese audience. Your tone should be humble. Your conduct should be modest; showy personalities are not appreciated in China, as this behavior would make your Chinese audience feel uncomfortable. Some "personality" is considered okay, but do not overdo it. Your speaking volume should be somewhere between the low to middle range. Speaking too loudly will also lead to a sense of discomfort among your listeners. You will also need to observe formalities of showing respect for established hierarchies and deference to seniority. In practical terms this means, for example, greeting the senior member of the team first when entering a room. You should dress professionally, but nothing more. Looking too good will automatically make others look bad, which is a potentially face-losing scenario for your hosts.

Experience has shown the author that the Chinese do indeed welcome and appreciate humor – especially humorous comments based on the immediate context. This is especially welcomed by lower-level engineers or by a relatively homogenous group where the top bosses are absent. If you inject a little humor here and there that is "safe" (i.e. not directed at any one person or cultural group specifically) then it should be okay.

Unlike many task-oriented cultures, the Chinese like to hear something about your company (its history, tradition and reputation) in some depth. They also want to hear about your department and how you fit into the company.

Opening structure

Right from the start, you will need to show your Chinese audience the outline of your presentation (i.e. the points you will be covering). This includes setting the *background context* before moving on to the core of your talk. Though it may sound needlessly explicit, it will be important for you to be as exact as possible.

An example would be:

- Introduction (company, personal)
- Background context
- Topic 1: Title
- Topic 2: Title
- Topic 3: Title
- Topic 4: Title
- Q&A
- End

After the introduction you should begin by setting the context of your presentation. Indeed, the one typical complaint that the

Chinese (as most other Asians) have of North American and Northern European presentations is that they come to the point too quickly, without explaining the necessary background context. Even in purely "product" presentations, for example, instead of talking directly about a new feature, the Chinese are also quite interested in learning about the circumstances (in some detail) that gave rise to the new feature.

Content and points of persuasion

You should not have to convince the Chinese that the quality of a product is good. They begin with this premise. If you emphasize too strongly that you have a high-quality product, they will begin to suspect the opposite and that you are hiding a defect.

Avoid comparisons with your competitors' products, which the Chinese would find inappropriate. If other products on the market are not able to fulfill a particular need, you can say, "we are the only ones able to offer this feature at the moment" (if true) or, "no one is able to offer this feature at the moment."

Demonstrating know-how is important to the Chinese. But you will not need an overly-detailed explanation on how something functions – as the Germans or Russians may require. This does not mean that they are not interested in the product per se. Indeed, they are good listeners and eager to learn as much as they can from those they think they can gain know-how from. But they are rather skilled at perceiving early on if a product or proposal is of interest to them. Too much depth (especially technical depth) is not desirable *early on*.

Just as important as explaining the features of a product is the need to communicate that you will be there and have time for them when they are ready to go deeper into the subject. You will need to communicate how *you* will help or advise them to achieve some objective. Communicate relationship - the longer the better. Of course, it's not enough to tell them, "We're interested in a long-term relationship". You will need to show what you mean by that and how specifically you've thought about it. They want to hear it. Even if your Chinese audience is only interested in licensing, they will still need to be satisfied that knowledge transfer will go smoothly – with very close cooperation along every step of the way.

Negative information or critique of any kind must be expressed indirectly to the Chinese. If you would like to express "no" or your disapproval for something, then it is enough to hesitate or vacillate on a point for your audience to interpret your real meaning. Nothing explicit needs to be said. And very importantly, no one should ever lose face.

The Chinese have a strong pragmatic side to them. They don't have to have the latest technological gimmick at any cost. If, for example, your technology is so sensitive that dust (with numerous dust storms in the north) may affect its performance, then they would rather have last year's model which is less sensitive. Therefore, if you must persuade, then look for genuinely pragmatic arguments to back up your positions.

In China, it is important to answer the question, "What happens if this product breaks down?" It might be the best quality on the market, but even the best sometimes break down. If there is no plan in your proposal to service and support your product, then it is unlikely they will be interested.

Unlike their Western counterparts, the Chinese do not appreciate listening to a presentation which offers countless options in product line or alternative solutions, *even if you have them*. They think that if you are the manufacturer then you should know what is best for their situation. If you have many options then you should make a case for one. *Usually, they like the standard one.* In a country their size, they think that if most people would want "X", then most people cannot be wrong.

Language must be broken down into small chunks – even for the translator. They cannot handle very long sentences, especially long or complex sentences filled with technical jargon. The presentation should be very clearly outlined. Tell them, "First, I will talk about this, then second, I will talk about that, etc." Using real-life examples and lucid analogies, in order to help visualize a vague concept, is very much appreciated in China.

Be careful with large numbers. The Chinese language only goes to ten thousand, after which multiples must be used. That means they need to calculate very large numbers in their heads. It would be a great help if large sums were just written out for them to see (e.g. 23,700,000). In addition, you should also be consistent with numbers when presenting to the Chinese. If you say 3,980, then later round it up to 4,000, they'll think you are inconsistent – and suspect you are trying to hide something. Numerical figures must be consistent. In those areas of your talk where you do need to make an estimate of some kind, then it is best to be cautious here. If you "estimate" that, in two years, you will get 80% of the market then the Chinese will hold you to those numbers. Therefore, it's better to just say something like, "we have a very good chance of succeeding". If, on the other hand, they try to get a specific numerical prediction from you, then make sure you qualify your figures with "if everything goes according to plan".

The Chinese often require a combination of graphics and text on slides. Graphics alone may not be enough as they will need an explanation of what you are trying to communicate to them. One should not let them try to determine the meaning of something on their own, as this does not reflect the learning style they have been brought up with. For the most part, the Chinese are not generally taught to think too abstractly or interpret meaning *on their own*. For example, in a strategy presentation given in China by the Swedish director of marketing for a Dutch electronics company, the picture of a shark swimming in the sea (the new market and labeled as such) was used to symbolize the dangers of entering this Chinese market, especially the tough competitors they would be facing. Afterwards, many of the participants approached the speaker and asked what the shark in the picture was supposed to mean. Some of them interpreted the shark quite literally, and hoped that this poor director did not think his competition was connected to the fish industry. Therefore, you will need to be explicit and exact with what you want, expect, or offer to do.

This tendency for the Chinese to take things literally should be kept in mind at all times, and you should adjust your communication accordingly. As for text slides, be careful here as well. The Chinese, like most Asian cultures, are much better at reading English than speaking and listening to it. If you show text slides they will find it easier to just read the slides and dispense with listening to you altogether. You will not only lose the human contact, but also the nuances in message and meaning (rarely captured in text slides) will be lost. They will, however, appreciate it if you write down the main ideas of your presentation and provide them as handouts in advance. The more pages contained in your handout, the earlier they should receive it (and a Chinese translation of it would be considered the ultimate aid).

The summary

There is no real summary to speak of in Chinese presentations. It is very important, however, that any questions that were raised *before* the talk be answered completely during the presentation. A desirable ending, therefore, would be to list the important questions with their concise responses for the audience to look at one last time. If you want to stress a key message, then it is best not to save it for the end, but to repeat your main point throughout the talk and in different ways.

Q&A

Finally, the Chinese consider it bad manners to interrupt during a presentation. Those who studied and worked in the West may be willing to interrupt if invited to do so. However, for the majority of the Chinese, you will not need to ask if they have any questions during your talk as they most likely won't ask, anyway. Rather, make sure you announce that you will leave time at *the end* for questions. After the official question period is over, however, do not just leave. Be willing to stay - as you will probably get another set of questions during this informal period as well.

III. Dos and Don'ts

With regard to presentations, the Chinese need or like:
- A clear outline
- An extensive background context
- A long-term view in your presentation
- Information about how you will help or advise them
- Communication of relationship
- Indirect communication when expressing "no" or something disliked
- Demonstration of know-how
- Respect for elderly and those in a senior position
- Modesty
- A humble tone
- Pragmatism in your ideas
- Occasional humorous comments
- Large numbers written out
- Absolute consistency with use of numbers
- A key message that is tightly linked to the information given

- Questions at the end – and then remain for yet another round of informal questions

...and they don't need or like:

- Loud or otherwise overwhelming personalities
- To interpret ideas that are not explicit

- Too much technical detail at the beginning
- Too many options

5

Making Presentations
in France

I. Presentation Profile - France

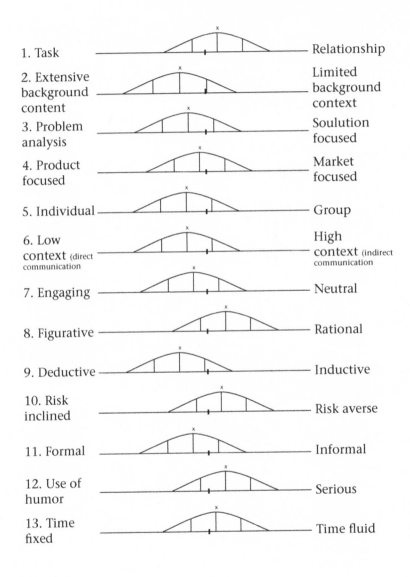

1. Task — Relationship

2. Extensive background content — Limited background context

3. Problem analysis — Soulution focused

4. Product focused — Market focused

5. Individual — Group

6. Low context (direct communication — High context (indirect communication

7. Engaging — Neutral

8. Figurative — Rational

9. Deductive — Inductive

10. Risk inclined — Risk averse

11. Formal — Informal

12. Use of humor — Serious

13. Time fixed — Time fluid

II. Exposé –
Making Presentations in France

First things first

Establishing a good relationship is a prerequisite to doing business in France. They not only want to know you as an individual, which takes time, but they want to be able to predict how a person will behave in a number of circumstances. The French are a bit distrustful of new contacts at first, but will give you a chance to prove yourself. Again, this will take time, so you might as well enjoy the process. If, in the end, they feel they can trust you then they'll proceed to the next step. If not, then they'll most probably avoid doing business with you – thinking, "Thank God, I don't have to work with that idiot". If an American did not like the person he was doing business with, he would say, "He's a jerk, but at least I got the business".

Things that will win you points are: to show you are well-mannered, not loud and boorish, cultured, and can speak French. Though fluency in French is no longer a prerequisite for international business people coming to France, one should at least know some survival phrases as well as something about France to avoid making a very bad impression. To a large degree, one must first begin by selling oneself. But this is not in the American sense, which is based on talking about yourself and what you can do or have done – a type of embarrassing self-promotion in the eyes of the French. Rather, it is based on what is observed over time: your sense of style, charm and savoir faire – as well as your manners, your ability to talk with genuine interest on a wide range of topics, your willingness to develop a relationship and your professionalism. The French need to *see* it, not just hear about it from your own lips.

An important area of trust-building for the French is for them to see that you are honest with your ideas and opinions. They then assume that when it comes to business you'll be straight with them. Therefore, one does not need to cultivate harmony with the French as is often the case in the Anglo-Saxon world. They like to see that you have your own opinion on a topic – even if they don't agree with you. They enjoy lively conversation and can be quite frank in their manner of disagreement with you, though they will never bully someone who holds a counter opinion. And there is almost no topic that is taboo (except talking about business during lunch). You will need to express yourself well – with wit and élan but, at the same time, without being argumentative.

The Presentation

The speaker

In France, speakers must be absolutely competent in their field. Usually they are older but, if not, then certainly mature in manner, well-dressed, refined, and with a broad range of knowledge. You must gauge your level of formality according to who makes up your audience. Those higher up in the hierarchy will require more formality and sophistication from the speaker. With young engineers you can be rather less formal in France today, but you should still be professional and avoid trying to win them over with self-deprecating remarks. Such humor is not considered endearing to the French.

The opening structure

To really understand any idea or any proposal, the French first require a well-constructed background as a setting for the topic. They do not want you to come "straight to the point". They have to know the circumstances that led to the present situation, from all angles. And they have to know that *you* know as well. Otherwise, they will think that any subsequent discussion on the topic will be faulty. It is the first step in a logical presentation. There can be no proper discussion of "what to do" before one first understands the "why" behind it. The relationship of cause and effect cannot be broken. A few sentences will not suffice here. It must be a richly woven picture which allows the listener to see the context clearly. Most Germans, Dutch and Americans would become impatient with the time needed for this part. But, for the French, one must always take as much time as needed to understand a situation completely.

Content and points of persuasion

French listeners expect to hear a discussion on any topic with an examination of the generalities first before moving on to specifics. For example, you may title a presentation, *"How to give presentations to the British"*. The suggestions on how to do this specifically will most likely only take up a fifth of the presentation content – and then *only at the end*. First, you would have to discuss how to look at culture in general, and then you would need to say something about the theory of communication, followed by a look at how culture manifests itself in communication – which, subsequently, would lead to an analysis of what historical factors influenced British culture and so on. You would then conclude by demonstrating how the various input strands of your discussion merge together to form the resulting hypothesis of your proposal. Finally, based on the resulting hypothesis, you would then proceed to make concrete suggestions. True, it is a circuitous approach, but one that is consistent with the Latin mind. If you want to persuade the French, you will need to consider their mode of thinking almost more than any argument points you come up with.

Speculative thinking is also an important element in getting the French to go along with you. It's not speculation based on intuition, but rather one that is "ultra" rationally informed. It's part of the Cartesian method which requires that all elements of a problem and its solution be mapped out before any action can be taken. Conceptual control is the overriding concern which, once established, permits one to act. For example, French chemists will speculate and discuss the probable outcome of a new formula before testing it while, more inductive-oriented cultures, such as in the United States, will first test it and then discuss the results. In any case, to suggest an action before all the various aspects of a situation have been presented will lead to near unanimous resistance in France.

As a culture, the French are usually cynical about new claims and new ideas. It's an attitude that is common to most Latin-Mediterranean countries. These cultures have been around for a while and they have seen and heard just about everything in their history, so you start off at a deficit. Therefore, you will need to spend extra time examining and supporting ideas and their application(s).

On the other hand, the French are relatively open, enthusiastic and highly respectful of new technology, especially sophisticated technology. They, in comparison with most Europeans, are "early adopters" and often accept the latest gadgets before their neighbors. They love innovative products which should have a practical application, be user-friendly and stylishly designed. The product will be even more highly considered if it is also "sympathique" (with a likable or congenial quality).

That said, you will still need to make product presentations relevant to the French culture. They need to hear how a product has been adapted to their realities – and why you think it will succeed in France. Be specific and make sure you support your claims.

Speakers must avoid exaggerated enthusiasm. Hyping a product (the best, the greatest, the newest) will only draw their attention in the opposite direction - to its possible flaws. Another reason "hype" is frowned upon in France is because it comes across as childish, as a form of pleading your position – which is considered inappropriate – and somewhat embarrassing for adults to engage in. Therefore, avoid exaggeration or any kind of hard sell in your presentation. This does not mean, however, that one should be stiff in one's delivery style. One should avoid coming across as monotone, rigid, or sounding too objective. Your personality should come through and you should speak as freely as possible. To the French, a scripted presentation (which includes reading from your PowerPoint slides) indicates unfamiliarity with the topic – and the speaker will lose points here.

The word "new" or "change" does not have the same appeal in France that it does with Americans. Product changes will be more acceptable if you use phrases like "developed further", "modernized" or "further refined".

Try to avoid stating the obvious to your French audience. They are especially critical of a presenter who feels compelled to mention something that, to them at least, would be self-evident. For example, if you say, *"the new microprocessor is twice as powerful as the previous generation"*, you will not need to add *"…and that means your current programs will run faster"*. They perceive this as being talked down to - and it can immediately turn them off to a speaker.

Summary and conclusion

The conclusion is very important in French presentations. The presentation needs to be brought together elegantly and rationally in a way that emphasizes the main objective of the whole talk. It is the "Grand Finale" during which your audience hopes you will tie your information together in way that provides a novel insight into the information you presented. Remember that stressing your main point at the beginning, as is the case in Anglo-American presentations, runs the risk of it being overlooked. A French audience may simply not hear it because they don't expect it at the beginning. Rather, it would be a good idea to quickly repeat the essence of each major thread and then interpret what it all means in a strong statement. For example, *"...now, because we've seen that natural resources are diminishing worldwide, and because we have shown that environmental laws for recycling are becoming more prolific in nearly all developed economies, and because we've also seen the nearly universal trends among those under 30 to use significantly less paper than older demographic groups, and since we have proven that all these trends will only accelerate exponentially in the next decade... we predict that hardcopy sales will drop to below a few thousand readers and, therefore, strongly recommend that you cease hardcopy publication of your magazine and move completely to an online format within the next three years"*.

Q&A

Expect to have some of your points challenged by the audience during your presentation. There is a twofold reason for this. First, your French audience may simply disagree with your facts or logic. Therefore, you should double check all your data – and have additional primary data available - *before beginning*. Secondly, it may be done to provoke further clarification. Contradiction, discussion, arguing and debate – in a public forum - are not seen as behaviors to avoid (for fear of disturbing group harmony) but as necessary activities to bring light into darkness and clarity into confusion. Speakers should not take the challenge personally. Indeed, you will win respect from the audience by answering well and showing that you enjoy the process.

Final points

It is best to avoid humor when giving a presentation in France. In the first place, the word humor in English is more closely associated with the word *mood* in French. Rather, French speakers appreciate the preferred (but only occasional) "witty" comment. If you can do this skillfully, without being sarcastic, then there is a chance you'll find a receptive audience. Otherwise, it is best to leave it out altogether.

Keep in mind that a specialist should never admit to not knowing something that is related to the topic, even if he or she doesn't know. If you don't know, it is expected that you give an intelligent answer - or talk around the question to something you do know. You will lose respect if you fail to appear fully competent in your field.

The French usually understand and *speak* English better than their popular stereotype would indicate. Nevertheless, it is still not at the very fluent level that most Northern Europeans have mastered. If you cannot speak French (very well) or do not have a French translator, then try to speak English as clearly as possible, free of any slang. Translating your talk into French and providing it as a handout will be much appreciated. Finally, avoid text slides in France. Although many speakers use them today, it does not mean that the audience likes this practice. Your diagrams should be as illuminating as your Cartesian logic. You will win many points by making your visuals clear and comprehensible.

III. Dos and Don'ts

With regard to presentations the French need or like:
- Competency of speaker in topic
- Logical arguments
- A well-developed background
- Points moving from the general to the specific
- Issues looked at from all relevant sides
- Ideas tied together in the conclusion
- Innovative and likable products
- Style, personal touch, formality
- Cultured speaker
- Your real opinion, lively discussion

...and they don't need or like:

- Hype or hyping
- Being spoken down to
- Getting straight to the point
- Superficial analysis

6

Making Presentations
in Germany

I. Presentation Profile - Germany

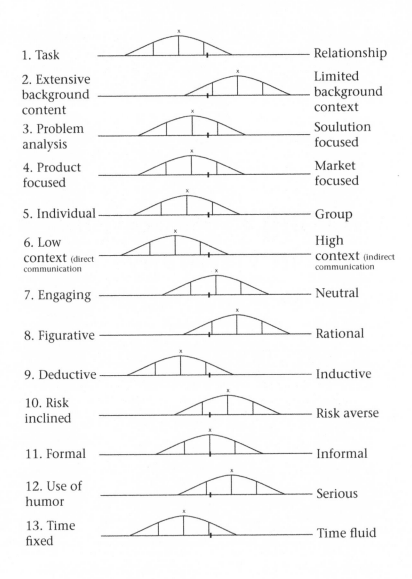

1. Task — Relationship

2. Extensive background content — Limited background context

3. Problem analysis — Soulution focused

4. Product focused — Market focused

5. Individual — Group

6. Low context (direct communication — High context (indirect communication

7. Engaging — Neutral

8. Figurative — Rational

9. Deductive — Inductive

10. Risk inclined — Risk averse

11. Formal — Informal

12. Use of humor — Serious

13. Time fixed — Time fluid

II. Exposé –
Making Presentations in Germany

First things first

No real relationship building phase is needed when doing business in Germany. It is a task and achievement-oriented culture that will examine any idea, product or service on its own merits. One should, however, be punctual for any appointment and be professionally dressed, though you should avoid being over-dressed or display personal jewelry ostentatiously. You should also maintain a professional and rather serious demeanor. Trying to win points by being chummy will probably backfire.

Though German businesses are in many ways *less* hierarchically structured than their US counterparts, there is still a level of formality that should be observed. Those with PhD titles (Doctors in German) should be addressed accordingly. Unless otherwise invited to do so, you should address your German contacts as Herr and Frau (last name), or Herr/Frau Doctor (last name).

Germany ranks as one of the top countries worldwide when it comes to the stress they put on punctuality. In business, even arriving a few minutes late (without a very good excuse) will create a bad impression. It is best, therefore, to be on time – and even better to arrive a few minutes early.

The Presentation

The speaker

The more formal qualification a speaker has (e.g. a PhD - especially in the area the topic will cover) the more credibility that person will have right at the start. In North America, experience trumps academic qualifications. In Germany, it is the other way around.

One's academic title, therefore, could be an important consideration when deciding who to choose to give the presentation.

German businesspeople do not expect or need you to create a
relaxed atmosphere before or during the presentation. They do require a serious and sober speaker who is absolutely competent in
the topic under discussion. The word "sober", however, does not
imply "dull". Germans do appreciate a genuinely good speaker,
one who can speak naturally and sound interesting while steering
clear of any *contrived* enthusiasm. A speaker who has a comfortable
tempo, good intonation, can pause in appropriate places and
sounds interesting will be highly valued. Though such speakers are
infrequent in German business circles, they are prized when effective delivery is combined with solid content.

Contrary to popular perception, Germans *do* have a sense of
humor, but it is not considered appropriate in the context of business. Indeed, it might even be perceived as a deficit to use humor
– in that a speaker would not appear "serious". Therefore, humor
and personal anecdotes are basically unnecessary to win over your
audience.

The opening structure

In many presentations around the world, Germany included, there
is often a difference between what audiences want and what speakers actually do. German presentations typically begin by stating
the topic they will be covering. This is not quite the same as a *purpose statement* which tells your audience exactly why you are there
and what you want to achieve. The rare speaker who includes both
the topic *and* purpose statement in the introduction, however, always gets a positive response from the audience.

Germans appreciate a well-outlined presentation (called an
Agenda in German) which can be quite extensive. It is not uncommon to have anywhere from 7-10 points on the "agenda", rather
than the 2-3 points typically found in Anglo-American outlines.

There is rarely a background context in German presentations. When it does appear it is usually a spontaneous insertion and very limited - not longer than a few sentences. Introducing a lengthy background, therefore, will most likely disorient your audience if it goes on for too long (more than 30 seconds). It might be best just to avoid it – or better, to avoid it *at the beginning*. A similar practice of "setting the scene" is often found in the first point of their outline where German presenters will "analyze the current situation".

Content and points of persuasion

For technical presentations, German audiences (remember, often made up of experts) like to see a picture of the product on a transparency or some equivalent (unlike the Japanese, who actually would prefer to handle it).

Germans respect simple honesty and directness. As a very low-context culture, they feel uncomfortable with indirectness or subtle nuances in meaning. Your message must be clearly spelled out and completely unambiguous. If you have something negative to say, then just say it. Your German audience can easily discern the difference between critical comment about a job poorly done and a personal attack. They will not confuse one for the other.

Germans tend to believe that Americans exaggerate and are happy with "superficial" presentations. This is because Germans are generally risk-adverse. They require quite a bit of information and detail, especially technical detail, to make a decision. One *cannot risk* leaving something important out. Sometimes, however, the love of details can cross the line into excess – with presentations that contain way too much information that is only indirectly related to the main topic. Even many Germans get impatient with their colleagues when they go overboard. This means you will need to edit yourself. Your talk can be meaty and detailed, but it should not be so for its own sake. On the other hand, take care not to go to the other extreme. If your content sounds too simple, with only a watered-down analysis of the situation, then you will be perceived as being unprepared – which is a definite minus.

When examining a solution (to whatever), you will need to begin with a thorough analysis of the problem. It is similar to the background information which sets the context of the talk. But in Germany, it is usually inserted as the first point of the main topics to be covered in the presentation (e.g. *"I've divided my presentation into three main topics. First, I will examine the current situation* (the classic German background). *After that, we will look at how we dealt with this problem. And finally, I will show you how this solution can be integrated into our current processes without much disruption"*). Your audience will need to see in clear steps how you arrive at your conclusions. Indeed, the emphasis on analysis is so strong in Germany that one wonders if the expression "paralysis through analysis" was not invented for them.

The attention to detail reflects the Germans' respect for thoroughness. They do not just want to know *what* something does; they want to know *how* it does it. They are process-oriented, with a deductive mode of thinking. They want to know how you arrived at your conclusions and if the analysis was sound. Planning must be thorough and consider *all* eventualities. Nothing should be left to chance.

Germans are "rational" in their expression. The use of examples and analogies is not typically a part of their communication pattern. They expect you to explain things clearly, without having to use many examples and analogies. A few are okay, but if you use more than a few, they will interpret it as your needing to speak down to them.

Germans will also listen critically, scanning your talk for inconsistencies and errors or for exceptions to any claim you may make. They generally feel uncomfortable with partial truths, believing that, if something is not 100% true, then it cannot be true at all.

They seek certainty, often by scanning their minds for exceptions to what you are claiming. This can be partly attributed to their society's strong inclination to avoid risk and ambiguity of any kind, and to their history of excelling in disciplines that call for measurable exactness (engineering, chemistry, physics and mathematics). If you are going to present a finding that is "generally" true, then you will need to first prepare the audience, showing them that you are aware that it is only a general finding and by no means universal. To gain respect, and to keep your audience from turning against you, you should also talk about some of the exceptions to the general rule you are proposing. See it as a preemptive strike against being perceived as saying something that isn't one hundred percent exact.

There should be no trace of trying to pitch or market your product with a *hard sell*. Otherwise, German audiences will think you are hiding something. Rather, a product should be able to speak for itself and be good enough to meet the German high standards for excellent quality. Indeed, in any product presentation, quality is probably the decisive factor. It must be soundly engineered, solid and well-built. This perception of solidness cannot be neglected in products. For example, in the early 90s, a Japanese electronics company introduced a new hi-fi tuner of superior quality and performance level. The tuner, however, did not sell well in Germany because it was considered too light in weight by the mostly male consumers of hi-fi equipment. It wasn't until the Japanese company remedied the situation by adding a heavy metal strip on the inside (to give it the proper *feeling* of solidness) that sales began to take off.

Another factor in a product presentation should be cost – though it is rare that the average German company will look for the cheapest price – with the exception of the food industry. They understand that quality has a price. Time, however, is also a key concern. Whatever time you claim to be able to deliver, produce, or start something, you must keep to it. If you cannot keep your word, one probably written down in a contract, then you will not only be considered unprofessional, but you may even face legal action.

The summary

At the end of the presentation, Germans will almost always summarize their talk by displaying their key message(s) on a Power-Point slide. It is rare that these sentences are short and memorable, since the audience can get an electronic or hard copy of the talk if requested. But if you want to score a few extra points, then try to shorten them as much as possible, while keeping them meaningfully informative. Again, not many presenters are able to do this, but those who can, get a positive nod.

Q&A

In the question & answer follow-up discussion, German audiences can be very direct (almost hard) in the way they formulate questions, objections or contrary opinions. In those parts of your talk where inconsistencies or inaccuracies were perceived, Germans will not hesitate to point them out in front of the entire group. (Remember, that your audience often consists of experts in the topic area.) Tough questioning should not be taken as a personal attack, as it reflects an uncompromising search for clarity. If you feel the tone is too hard and heavy, then try to resist reacting defensively. The audience would very likely be puzzled by such a response. Rather, try to overlook it and just answer the question professionally and dispassionately.

Final Points

The business dress code in Germany will vary depending on who your audience is. You should always dress professionally. The one exception is with engineers, who will require a semi-casual dress look (e.g. a not too flashy coat with jeans, a shirt with collar, and polished shoes is standard). No tie is needed in a technical presentation to engineers given by an engineer (or else the audience may suspect that you are not an engineer yourself). Otherwise, the higher up the hierarchical ladder you go, the darker the suit must be (though black is uncommon). Men should also avoid wearing jewelry beyond the wedding band and watch (which shouldn't look cheap). Women should also wear a business suit with blouse and fine nylons (avoid embroidered designs). Jewelry should be chic but understated. For both genders, the clothing should consist of natural materials (i.e. cotton, wool or silk). Synthetic fibers will be noticed and probably make a bad impression.

III. Dos and Don'ts

With regard to presentations Germans need or like:
- Sober and professional speaker
- Clear structure
- An outline (agenda) of the points you will be covering
- Technical expertise /qualified background of speaker
- Quality of your products
- Unambiguous communication
- More information rather than less
- A thorough analysis of existing problems and potential solutions
- Seeing how you arrived at your conclusions
- The chance to challenge a speaker strongly when necessary

...and they don't need or like:

- Style over content
- Too many analogies

- Flattery of any kind
- A superficial analysis

7

Making Presentations in India

I. Presentation Profile - India

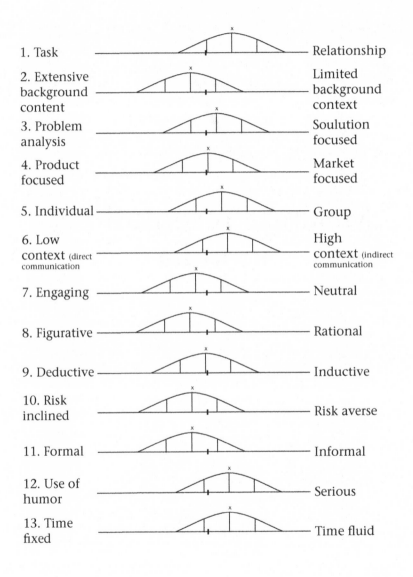

1. Task — Relationship

2. Extensive background content — Limited background context

3. Problem analysis — Soulution focused

4. Product focused — Market focused

5. Individual — Group

6. Low context (direct communication — High context (indirect communication

7. Engaging — Neutral

8. Figurative — Rational

9. Deductive — Inductive

10. Risk inclined — Risk averse

11. Formal — Informal

12. Use of humor — Serious

13. Time fixed — Time fluid

II. Exposé –
Making Presentations in India

First things first

Establishing a solid relationship is perhaps the key criterion for doing business successfully in India. The same goes for giving presentations. It's important to understand that everything you do – from the minute you enter, to the moment you leave, is considered *the presentation*. Building a solid relationship is considered more important than the content of a few presentations. The one who gives them should be someone who possesses finely-tuned social antenna and proper cross-cultural communication skills. The person will need to interact with and appreciate the culture, become acquainted with the Indian values system and respect the established hierarchy that exists in nearly every business. He will also need to know something about the importance of family (and talking about it), religion (not talking about it for the most part), and about India in general. Finally, developing trust should be a priority in relationship building. Indians will look at your demeanor (hopefully, calm and unforced), your desire to get to know them apart from doing business with them, your flexibility and patience, your trust in life and, lastly, your product and ideas if you're there on business.

You should avoid delicate discussion topics with your Indian hosts (e.g. the caste system, poverty, Pakistan, Kashmir, cows, child labor, arranged marriages, etc.). Indians are interested when you take a genuine interest in them, but may have a hard time answering difficult and "awkward" questions. It is important to make a clear distinction between genuinely asking open questions and *questioning something* (with its unpleasant whiff of judgement). One can easily observe the example of almost any Indian you encounter –

who seems to be ignorant to the latter possibility in his own inquiries.

India, running across all of its different cultural and language groups, is thoroughly hierarchical in its social structure. Therefore, when beginning a presentation, it is very important to wait until the most superior person in the group is present. Starting without this key decision-maker would be a serious mistake. And not having a key decision-maker in your audience is probably a waste of time. You will also need to demonstrate more respect to those at the higher end of the hierarchy (i.e. using their titles and last names, acknowledging them first when entering a room). In addition, avoid trying to bridge any established status distance through what would be considered informal behavior (e.g. touching beyond the hand shake, enquiring about personal information, joking around, or even positioning yourself in such way as to become the center of the group) as this will be viewed unfavorably.

The Presentation

The speaker

Regardless of the presentation content (academic or business), it is important to convey the impression that you have truly researched your topic well, that you are competent, that you have know-how. This does not mean that you engage in *information dumping*. Quantity is not equal to quality in India. It does mean that you select your information carefully – relevant to the topic – and provide a unique insight that others may have overlooked. Indians will be especially keen to hear it – and you will win their esteem if you can provide it.

You must avoid superficiality, as if the only thing you can offer is a polished sales pitch. Indians are particularly sensitive to being taken for granted. The country boasts very astute businessmen, distinguished academics and brainy scientists. So you risk underestimating them at your own peril. Your Indian audience will also be observing how well you relate as a person – and not just on the quality of your content. They should have the feeling that you are genuinely interested in them during the presentation and that they are more important than business. That interest, if successfully conveyed, will then be reciprocated.

Indians tend to be extroverted in their communication styles. They can be talkative, enjoy lively conversation, use body language expressively, and don't mind interruptions at all. In short, they are closer to Mediterraneans in communication style than to Northern Europeans. Presenters who enjoy speaking and can express themselves compellingly will have an advantage over the more introverted types.

Be aware of your body language in presentations to Indians. Speakers who move too much will come across as nervous or restless, in contrast to the composure Indians admire. This does not imply being stiff (or boring). It does mean showing expression that is natural but composed. Prolonged eye contact should be avoided as a sign of respect. It should never be intense. Rather, let it be brief (no more than a second). Indian audiences also prefer a speaking volume in the middle range. Not as loud as most Americans, but not as soft as the Japanese.

The opening structure

As in many relationship cultures, you will need to begin your presentation by providing a background to the topic under discussion. Building a necessary context of your talk includes illustrating the relationship between past and present, the problem and the proposed solution, the whole and its parts. It's like a compass which establishes the cardinal points of your talk. Without it, your listeners become disoriented and experience the nagging sensation of not being completely sure of the direction in which you're moving. Therefore, take the time to set the scene fully. If possible, do it in story form. It will not only aid memory but it will also conform to a learning approach, which is valued in Indian culture.

As for the purpose statement, one is free to place it just before the background story or immediately after it. But, again, keep in mind that the purpose of your talk is not completely dependent on how well you formulate it, but through the background as well, as stressed above.

It will be important to outline the main points of your talk as well, especially for those in the audience who either studied or worked in the West. Your list of "points to cover" should be limited in number (not exceeding 5 points) and be tied together in a logical flow.

Content and points of persuasion

In an Indian business context, a presentation should not be too densely loaded with information. Although Indian audiences, and especially those in technical fields, can handle rigorous, long and densely-packed presentations (hardened by years of training in their schools and universities), this approach would not be considered desirable in a non-university setting, and especially not in a business context. Technical presentations, on the other hand, are often overloaded with information the world over. But this is not because technical people, Indian or otherwise, necessarily learn more effectively through information dumping. It has more to do with a self-perpetuating "bad habit" of using presentation slides as documentation. Whether an audience can actually comprehend, let alone retain, any of the information with this practice is highly unlikely. It is okay to have detailed, text-based documentation as handouts, but you should only use clear slides that illuminate while presenting.

Indians are only somewhat interested in how things work. Rather, what a product or service does, and how it can be of value to them in their specific context, is what any product presentation should concentrate on in India. You will have to demonstrate that you indeed know their situation – the unpredictability of events - and provide broad contingencies.

Above all, the majority of Indians need to be given the big picture. This should not be confused with the background statement which establishes the context of your talk. Rather, the big picture is the general idea – or essence - of what you are striving to communicate. Similar to Americans, Indians will be motivated by your vision. If they sense an opportunity, they will go for it, even if all the details are not worked out. Indeed, they do not need or even want exhaustive details of a plan. They believe things will never go according to plan anyway. A general roadmap and a realistic understanding of the situation will suffice. A way will always be found to accomplish what needs to be done, through business and family connections, spontaneous creativity or simple fate. A solution, it is believed, will appear at the appropriate moment.

It is important that presenters appear genuinely motivated by their topic. However, you need to strike a balance here. In India, it is acceptable to display more confidence than in China or Japan, but not overly so. Exuberance must be tempered with modesty and humility. Indians, perhaps more than any other people in the world, are able to hold that tension between excitement and unflappable composure, between enthusiasm and serenity. It is an ideal that many Indian speakers seek to embody and see in others.

Most Indians appreciate and can listen at length to an articulate, eloquent speaker in English (free from slang and strong regional accents). Good storytellers who are able to convey a poignant wisdom, weaved seamlessly into their business or academic topic, will definitely be viewed highly. A favorite leitmotif is stories of people who were confronted and tested by fate but were able to meet it with profound wisdom and humility. Linked to this is a speaker's skilful use of metaphors, examples and analogies, all of which help build a picture in the mind. This skill is considered the mark of a good speaker in India.

Of course, price is an important factor in product presentations. They will expect the lowest possible quote. Products that require complicated logistical support will also have a hard time being accepted nationwide (with New Delhi, Mumbai and Bangalore being exceptions).

Reading excessively from a script or PowerPoint slide will give the impression that the speaker is unacquainted with the material. On the other hand, the ability to improvise or speak extemporaneously, yet remain confident and keep your ideas coherent, will be seen in a very positive light in India and should not be underestimated. It shows the audience that you know the topic well and that you're an expert. As a result, confidence in the speaker is strengthened which, in itself, is considered a persuasive argument. Of course, poise and confidence should be part of a larger "strategy of persuasion" which includes an interesting product or service, having the right partners, and understanding India's particular situation with all it entails: logistics, finance, the need to employ as many people as possible, and so on. The kind of confidence that is frowned upon, however, is that which seems contrived, forced and overly energetic. Rather, it should be a natural part of the speaker. It must flow naturally and come from a deep well of knowledge and experience.

Another quality that will greatly impress your Indian audience is the ability to think "out of the box" or come up with an improvised solution, even bending the rules if need be when circumstances demand it (known as *Jugaad*). This ability to be creatively flexible is highly esteemed. Therefore, you should not shy away from presenting out-of-the-box ideas to new and old challenges. Your audience will be eager to hear them.

Connected to out-of-the-box thinking is openness to new trends and new ideas. Indians do not mind hearing bold new claims, as long as they can be substantiated. Of course, it will help if you can quote a well-known authority that supports them.

In general, Indians are predisposed to taking risks, as they already believe life is full of uncertainties. One must learn to live with them and even demonstrate composure in the midst of them. If a business plan doesn't work out, then it is likely it wasn't meant to (kismet or karma). This attitude allows for a great deal of equanimity, and risk friendliness. As a result, failure is not considered a stigma; many lessons can be gained from the experience. Therefore, don't be afraid to share anecdotes in your presentation which illustrate some relevant learning point you gleaned from a disappointing venture.

India, with all its sub-cultures, is a collectivist society, though not as extreme as in East Asia. Still, one should do his or her best to avoid conflict. You should never cause an individual or group to lose face. Therefore, indirect communication is an important skill to develop. When speaking to a group, it's not a problem to point out "difficulties" in the process, production or strategy of your plan. But direct critique should be absolutely avoided. Whatever criticisms you do have should be conveyed in an indirect manner. For example, *"The software program was not able to accomplish all the tasks we thought it would – but it should be no problem, given the talent on our team, to add the necessary features"*. Remember, the stress in doing business in India is always on developing personal relationships. The link cannot be broken. Unlike many Northern Europeans and North Americans, who tend to compartmentalize tasks from relationships, most of the rest of the world *does not*. Criticizing the work is, first and foremost, seen as a critique of the person or group – which will weaken the relationship link. This does not mean that Indians cannot handle disappointment. Quite the contrary, they can handle it much better than most Westerners if communicated properly, so that face is not lost. A speaker should also be aware of not communicating negative information unconsciously by coming across as anxious, impatient, worried or aggressive. Remember to keep a sense of inward composure, a value Indians deeply admire.

The summary

A systematic summary of the main points in the body is usually not given in India. Ending your presentation should not be a drawn-out event. It is enough to quickly paraphrase why the presentation was important in the first place (e.g. "...so now we see why this would be a good area to invest in" or "...based on this research and analysis, it would seem that our only strategy is to change directions").

Q&A

For the most part, questions come at the end of a presentation in India. Time should be allotted for a Q&A session.

Final points

Humor in the work place is something some Indians are not used to. Though some westernized Indians may enjoy and practice it among those they consider their equals, it is best to be safe here and avoid using it in your presentation.

Bear in mind that head movement from side to side means "I'm listening".

When it comes to visual support in your presentation, Indians generally like clear and contrasting colors. Therefore, in designing your slides you should take this into consideration. You should also avoid too much text. In fact, you should reduce it to a minimum, but make sure you indicate that the full text is in the notes. Informative diagrams and pictures should be used more than bullet points. And keep in mind that even numbers are considered unlucky in India, whereas odd numbers bring luck.

Finally, deep within the Indian psyche is a profound respect for wisdom and astute perception embodied in the sage (the Guru). Be careful, however, of using the term "guru" lightly – as one often does in the West when referring to "the expert" in a given field. Instead, *quoting* a recognized expert will be viewed positively. In addition, quoting a poignant yet relevant saying from someone, perhaps from someone in your own culture, will be regarded highly. Of course, you don't want to overdo it; one or two references will be enough.

III. Dos and Don'ts

With regard to presentations Indians need or like:
- An eloquent and composed speaker who can speak freely
- Great competency in topic area
- Relevant story
- Quality information
- Tact
- Quotes from respected experts
- Examples, analogies, metaphors and anecdotes
- Visual support that is stimulating but makes complex ideas clearer
- Creative, out-of-the-box solutions, flexibility
- New trends and ideas supported by experts
- A humble tone
- Great lessons learned from failure

...and they don't need or like:

- Information dumping (needless quantity)
- Reading from a scripted text
- Agitated speakers
- Being underestimated

8

Making Presentations
in Israel

I. Presentation Profile - Israel

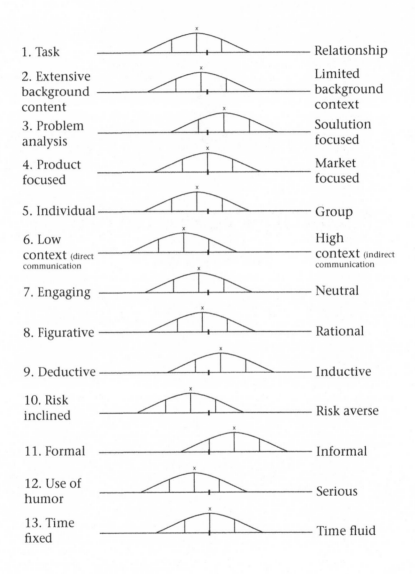

1. Task	Relationship
2. Extensive background content	Limited background context
3. Problem analysis	Soulution focused
4. Product focused	Market focused
5. Individual	Group
6. Low context (direct communication	High context (indirect communication
7. Engaging	Neutral
8. Figurative	Rational
9. Deductive	Inductive
10. Risk inclined	Risk averse
11. Formal	Informal
12. Use of humor	Serious
13. Time fixed	Time fluid

II. Exposé –
Making Presentations in Israel

First things first

Israel is a country largely made up of immigrants or children of immigrants (and a non-Jewish, mostly Palestinian-Arab population of nearly two million people) drawn from a Jewish diaspora of three groups (Ashkenazi, Sephardic and Mizrahi) spread across the world. Israeli communication styles, therefore, will reflect these cultures in all their disparities – from Russians (about 20% of the population) to Yemenis, Iranians to North Americans, Germans to Georgians, Argentines to Bulgarians and so on. Nevertheless, in spite of these differences, which cannot be overlooked among the immigrant groups, a general communication style among those born in the country has emerged. This profile will concentrate on the Israeli-born, Jewish population.

Israelis manifest aspects of both task and relationship attitudes in many areas of society and life. Take, for example, relationships. Israel is considered a relationship-oriented culture by many intercultural experts. There is a need to engage with the person in doing business and not just keep a formal distance. And yet, the way they go about establishing these relationships has strong elements of the non-relationship, task-oriented cultures. They can be direct and brusque, often disregarding the niceties associated with relationship-building – sometimes not even shaking hands. They are also critical of vagueness (common in relationship cultures) when giving or listening to negative information.

In Israel, it's important to be outgoing, candid and approachable. Visitors should learn some words in Hebrew (which is not biblical Hebrew). It's also essential to demonstrate a little self-deprecating humor and not take yourself too seriously. If Israelis perceive even a whiff of arrogance in you, they will turn off quickly and may even try to undermine you. This is rooted in the socialist egalitarianism of Israel's early founders and settlers. Israel is quite different today, with less economic egalitarianism noticeable compared to even the 70s and 80s. However, social and interpersonal attitudes are still conspicuously informal. The interaction between the powerful and not so powerful is not only possible, but is also considered desirable. In an informal culture like that found in Israel, the movement from complete stranger to intimate acquaintance can occur rapidly.

The Presentation

The speaker

In Israel, a presenter should be uninhibited and self-confident, but not arrogant. He should be *very competent* in the topic under discussion. Indeed, the topic should be so much a part of the speaker that he can relax and even have fun with it. In addition, he should be authentic, honest and able to say exactly what's on his mind. In other words, he should be a bit tough. But, even though Israelis like to see someone that is slightly rough around the edges, they also want to see some humanness in the speaker, someone who can share something personal about himself as well. Most of all, he should have a sense of humor.

As a presenter, you will need to find the middle ground with regards to delivery style. You shouldn't be too neutral (lacking expression) or what Israelis would call boring. But you should not be overly charismatic or emotional, either. The personality needs to show through but not be a distraction.

The opening structure

You should announce what you are going to talk about *specifically* (e.g. "I'd like to talk to you today about successful strategies for

Internet advertising in three different budget categories..." and not "I'd like to talk to you about Internet advertising"). Generalities and vagueness are not welcomed. Israelis, perhaps more than any other cultural group, easily become impatient (and sometimes vocal) if they are not clear about what specifically you want to tell them.

There should not be too much non-essential information in your presentation. Basically, you need to get to the talk quickly without a detailed introduction or in-depth history of your company. This does not mean that you are to rush through your presentation. It does mean, rather, that you can begin straight away with a related anecdote or short background story that brings your listeners immediately into your presentation topic. Israelis require a certain amount of background context, enough to put them solidly in the picture. The audience will want to know what the situation is.

What you cannot do is begin your presentation by reading bullet points to them. This would end in disaster. Israelis like someone who can "speak freely" (without the aid of extensive notes or bullet points). You should be able to speak to your audience as if you were having an interesting discussion with them. Tying your ideas into a story form or a string of related anecdotes would be viewed positively. Again, the anecdotes should be meaningful and even contain important facts, hard data and quotes from experts – all of which are woven together to create an interesting narrative the audience can follow.

In business presentations, there should be a light structure. This is not because Israelis have a strong need for order, which they don't, but because it is to ensure that the *speaker* keeps from digressing. In addition, your audience will also be able to hear (or see) in your outline what points you intend to cover - and reserve the option to change your content if needed *on the spot.*

Content and points of persuasion

For product presentations, simply offering a product or service similar to one that already exists will not impress an Israeli audience. To get your audience's attention, you will need to stress a *significant improvement* made to it. You will need to show clearly how it is better and more useful than that of a previous model or of a competitor's. The argument cannot be made through clever discourse but through something tangible. Israelis are some of the most pragmatic people in the world, with a strong aversion to ideas that have no practical application. They are more interested in "what" rather than "how" something functions. "How" is only of interest when what you are proposing presents acknowledged developmental or implementation roadblocks.

If there is a problem to which you are proposing a solution, then briefly go over the problem first so that the issue is clear. It should descriptive enough to give your listeners a good solid picture of the situation. But be careful not to overdo it. Analyses that are too long-winded will stir your audience to impatience. It is with the solution (or proposal) that you will need to spend some time and analysis. Keep in mind that almost any solution or proposal, except for infrastructure projects, which require long-term investments of time, money and resources will not be of much interest to them.

Israelis very much appreciate learning something new. It can be a unique insight into an old problem, an innovative solution never thought of before, or just an interesting related fact. Knowledge is an important value; interesting knowledge is even better; and interesting and useful knowledge is the ultimate. Without this "added feature" in your presentations, your listeners will think something was missing in your talk.

Similar to Italy and Brazil, the ability to be flexible, to improvise and to creatively adapt to sudden changes is a particularly admired quality in Israel. Indeed, it is seen as a critical survival element and, therefore, must be built into the plans you offer. Plans are not seen as a target to fulfill but as a starting point to build on.

To most Israelis, risk is a part of life and certainly a part of business. Those who are aware of the risks involved in a proposal, and can articulate them, will be seen as more credible. So, rather than try to cover up risk or downplay it, it would be wise if part of your presentation dedicates some time to examining the risks involved.

Likewise, playing things too safe or staying within the prescribed way of doing things is not considered inherently good in Israel – and can even make a bad impression. You should test the edge of what is possible and bend the rules creatively where you can. For example, if you are analyzing a problem you stand a better chance of being heard by presenting a creative solution, ideally requiring a minimum of resources, than offering a standard solution that brings little gain. Keep in mind, however, that you will still need to back up your idea with hard facts and solid data.

Israelis will openly challenge you if what you say is not confirmed by *their* experience. They are not impressed by good arguments – no matter how logical they may appear to be. Arguments, therefore, must be solidly grounded in reality, in experience, and in an intuitive common sense – which are considered important measures of truth.

Israel is considered a low-context culture. Negative information, therefore, can be given directly, though it should not appear as personal criticism. Only hinting at a problem is not enough and will confuse your audience and lead to scepticism about you and your product/service. In addition, slides should also be clear and to the point. Busy slides may provoke suspicion, as if you are deliberately trying to hide something in the details.

The summary

In Israel, the summary and concluding remark should be given proper attention when developing your presentation. You should distil the essential points of your talk into a few key summary points (review of the vital information) and then link them at the end with a key message that is clear and concise. Nothing should be left open to interpretation. You can also follow your key message with a short anecdote or statement to think about (known as a "concluding remark"), one that will not only get your audience to reflect, but one that also inspires action.

Q&A

In the question and answer section of your presentation (during or at the end), do not take it personally if you are strongly challenged by your audience – not just with questions but also with opposing opinions. Challenging authority is an acceptable code of conduct in this strongly egalitarian society. Israelis can appear very upfront, almost tactless, lacking many of the softeners typically demonstrated in Anglo-Saxon countries. This direct, straight-talk is known as "dugri talk" in Israeli slang. But it is not considered negative. Rather, it is associated with truthfulness and transparency.

Final points

Dressing in Israel is for the most part casual – though this is also changing. In the past, even the Israeli Prime Minister would come to his office in a short sleeve shirt and without a necktie. Today, you will need to consider the industry (if in business) or the group (e.g. engineers or board members) to whom you will be giving your presentation. One thing is still pretty certain though – you should not overdress. You can be professional, but you shouldn't overdo it. And, in after-business situations, Israelis tend to be quite casual in their style of dress.

III. Dos and Don'ts

With regard to presentations the Israelis need or like:
- A competent and self-confident speaker
- A speaker who is honest and says what's on his mind
- Informality
- A speaker who speaks without notes
- A specific topic
- The essential information
- What the situation is, the background context given clearly and concisely
- Facts, hard data, "what" more than "how"
- Meaningful anecdotes, a story
- Flexibility, creativity and innovativeness in your ideas
- An opportunity to learn something new and useful
- Directness
- The chance to challenge the speaker if necessary
- A clear summary and thought provoking conclusion

...and they don't need or like:

- Someone who takes himself too seriously
- Vagueness
- Confusing and cluttered slides
- Purely logical arguments

9

Making Presentations
in Italy

I. Presentation Profile - Italy

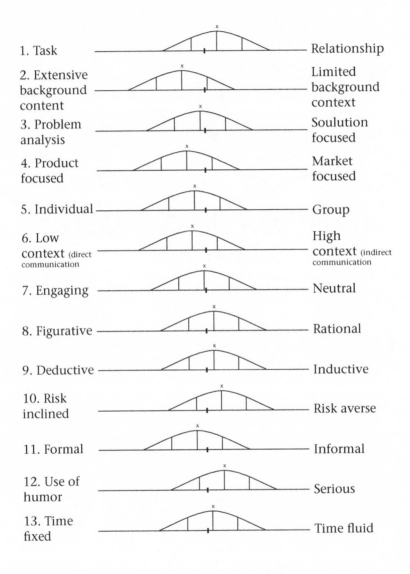

1. Task — Relationship

2. Extensive background content — Limited background context

3. Problem analysis — Soulution focused

4. Product focused — Market focused

5. Individual — Group

6. Low context (direct communication — High context (indirect communication

7. Engaging — Neutral

8. Figurative — Rational

9. Deductive — Inductive

10. Risk inclined — Risk averse

11. Formal — Informal

12. Use of humor — Serious

13. Time fixed — Time fluid

II. Exposé –
Making Presentations in Italy

First things first

Establishing a relationship is a prerequisite to doing business in Italy. Italians not only want to know you as an individual, but they will want to know about your company as well. Of course, all of this will take time because Italians need to know if they can really do business with you – and, if you can do business with them. There will be many starts and stops and restarts. Patience is a main ingredient for doing business there. And the further south you go, the more patience is required, as things usually take more time. In the North, business is a fine-tuned machine. Relationships are important. Tapping into a network of connections is valuable. But what you know and what you can do are of equal importance – especially in Milan. New ideas may need some time to consider, but once a decision is made plans will be implemented relatively quickly. In Milan and Turin, time is tight. In the South, it's different; making decisions and implementing plans will take much longer and will depend on the relationships you have developed.

One quality that Italians find essential and value greatly, both in business and personally, is flexibility. Where Germans want to plan for change, Italians seek to *respond* to change. The ability to adapt to new circumstances will win you respect *and* trust. Those who come from cultures that value sticking to the "agreed upon contract" - no matter how much the circumstances have changed - will provoke a deep mistrust in their Italian counterparts. The chances are that you will not develop a long-term business relationship – if at all.

103

In general, presentations are not a preferred practice in Italy. Rather, Italians much prefer a discussion format to gather information, where they can ask questions and make comments. Italians will listen to business presentations and sometimes even give them, but all in all they don't – as a culture - put much weight on them. They simply recognize that as business becomes more international, they will need to adapt to the new rules of the game. That said, what should one consider when making a presentation in Italy?

The Presentation

The speaker

Contrary to popular stereotypes, most Italians do not like to see theatrical presentations in the context of business. Long-winded yet eloquent speakers belong to the realm of political speech-giving or TV talk shows where personal opinions are freely indulged. Business presentations, on the other hand, demand more sobriety. Primarily, a speaker should be prepared and knowledgeable (which is not the same as being competent in Italy). You should demonstrate that you really know what you're talking about, and you should be able express yourself clearly and compellingly.

A good speaker shouldn't be monotone, but also not too theatrical. Italians will find it quite offensive if they perceive you are being dramatic or gesticulating eccentrically in order to accommodate some stereotype you have of them. They want a speaker to appear confident but not arrogant. You need to give the audience the assurance that they're in good hands, with your confidence based in knowledge and experience. It will also be a plus if a speaker is "simpatico" (friendly, approachable and flexible), especially with mid-level management and below. This does not mean, however, that you should be too chummy with your Italian counterparts. With upper-level management you will need to keep a bit of distance and show deference. Whatever the profile of the audience, you should avoid telling jokes as it is usually considered inappropriate and, somehow, not stylish.

The opening structure

Company history and reputation are important in Italy. If you are "unknown", you will need to talk about your company at the beginning of your presentation and assure your audience that you have good products or services. As Italians are somewhat risk averse, they will need to know that you have a solid enterprise behind you. If you have a proven record of being able to adapt quickly to changing circumstances, it would be advantageous to point that out. Remember, flexibility is a highly regarded quality in Italy – especially in business.

After announcing the topic of your presentation, most Italian presenters move right into developing the background in some detail. Similar to the French, there can be no discussion about what to do or about a new product before one fully understands the contextual situation behind it - with all relevant aspects. You will need to strike a balance here between not going on too long and being complete. As for stating the *main objective* of the talk, it is rarely done at the beginning – if at all. It is sort of implicitly understood what the presentation is (or should be) aiming to accomplish. Sometimes, it cannot even be articulated by Italian speakers themselves. For practical purposes, however, it is best to state the objective at the beginning and at the end in the concluding remark (see below: The summary).

The flow of the presentation does not have to be completely linear to Italian audiences. It should not be so structured that all spontaneity is organized out of it; there should be some flexibility built into the structure. That means you should have a basic outline, but nothing so finely divided and sub-divided that you lose the "talking-to-your-audience" feel of your presentation. Digressions are very much allowed and enjoyed, as long as they're meaningful, interesting and reconnect back to the main thread of your talk.

Content and points of persuasion

Like other Mediterranean cultures, Italians feel more comfortable talking about generalities first and "details" afterwards. The details, however, should never be exhaustive. They should be presented only as support to your general idea. Presenting details for details' sake (i.e. too much information), especially in a business context, will only get on their nerves. This is not the case, however, when explaining processes where members of your Italian audience will be involved (in carrying out those processes). In this case, a specific explanation of each step will be required. They will most likely make changes to the process (and plans), but it is important for them nonetheless to see you've thought about it first.

In a business-presentation context, Italians do not like a speaker to engage in too much theorizing. You should stay with the concrete and pragmatic. They are basically intolerant of abstractions and can be cynical when it comes to idealistic proclamations of any kind or statements with superlatives in them. More than any other culture in the West, Italians will doubt first, and only through an arduous process of persuasion let themselves be convinced of an idea. In order to convince them, they will first need to understand the big picture which, in many cases, means how they can profit in an Italian context. It will help if they see you've had success elsewhere – but they will then want to see how the plan can be adapted to their situation. Financing will also need to be addressed.

For a product presentation, Italians are especially interested in its engineering and design. Consumer products should not only be practical, but they should appear "congenial and attractive". They also want to see how products and services can be adapted to their specific situation, which is something you will have to research thoroughly.

Italians are equally balanced between the purely rational and figurative in their communication style. They can easily handle sublime ideas but also like to hear very specific and concrete examples. They use analogies occasionally but it is not a salient feature of their communication style.

As in most countries in Europe, speakers must avoid exaggerated enthusiasm. Hyping a product will provoke feelings of profound skepticism – especially among the management class in Italy. They may challenge a speaker here. They will not, however, intentionally try to embarrass you or trap you. The focus will be on the claim and not the speaker.

Civilization on the Italian peninsula is old by any standard. And the people there have seen everything in the form of movements, ideas, experiments, invading armies and personalities come and go. That's why Italians have become distrustful of absolutism in any form. Rigid thinking leads to rigid interpretations of reality, which inevitably leads to rigid solutions for rigidly-defined problems. Therefore, any attempt to persuade with clever arguments with tight tolerances will not get you far with an Italian audience. You must demonstrate flexibility in your attitude and approach to problems.

The word "new" or "changed" does not have the same appeal to Italians as with North Americans. With such adjectives Italians may ask, "What was wrong with it? Was it defective?" It's better to avoid provoking such questions by using phrases like "developed further", "modernized" or "further refined". These are terms that express continuity (considered desirable) rather than an abrupt change (undesirable).

For academic presentations, Italians usually pull a page out of their university experience. Most examinations in the university are given orally - where a student is usually required to demonstrate as much knowledge as he possesses about a subject – citing experts along the way. There is no attempt to be enthusiastic, entertaining or polished. What counts is the quality of information given. This style pervades most non-business-related scientific and academic talks. And, to some degree, it spills into numerous technical and business presentations given within companies. This is not to say that your presentation should adhere to this style. Indeed, most Italians would prefer that it didn't. They appreciate good speakers who can hold their attention with an interesting topic. As stated above, it need not be overly emotional (in style) to move and inspire them.

Italians have a strong aversion to losing face in public. Criticism should never be directed at anyone in particular. You will need to learn how to talk about a problem without talking about the agent. Likewise, a speaker, supposedly informed about his topic, should never be in a position where he says "I don't know". This is one of the many ways you can "fare una brutta figura" (cut a bad figure). If you do not know the answer to a question, you will be expected to give an intelligent response anyway. This does not hold true for minor facts and data (e.g. numbers) which are not immediately at hand. You can always indicate that you will get back to them with the exact data.

One aspect of the Italian communication pattern is to hear important ideas repeated a number of times. Italians will listen politely but not always pay full attention to an important statement, as they will expect the speaker to repeat it again in a slightly different way. And they will expect it from you as well. It would also help to find a picture or use some diagram that captures your main idea. You can forget a PowerPoint text slide, as they probably won't read it if it is overly-packed with words. In a country that excels at design like few others, they will appreciate a nicely illustrated diagram or image that anchors itself easily to memory.

The summary

The conclusion is more than just a place to repeat your main points in an Italian presentation. Rather, it is the place "to make your point". The presentation needs to be brought together elegantly and rationally in a way that punctuates the main objective of the *whole* talk. At the beginning of the presentation, Italians mention what they are going to talk about as a kind of title to their presentation. But it is at the end where all the ideas in the talk are tied together and make a grand conclusion, where the picture you have been painting finally makes sense.

Q&A

Questions may be asked during the presentation, depending on either who you are or the content of your topic. It is a good idea, nevertheless, to leave time at the end for further questions. It is in the Q&A stage that Italians come into their own, where they feel most comfortable. This is partly because they do not view the Q&A phase strictly as such. Rather, they see it more as a discussion period – sometimes lively - where they will be able to comment and discuss and not just have questions answered. You will need to be prepared. If no questions are asked or no comments made, then it is probably a bad sign. It may indicate that they are not interested or that they did not understand the presentation at all.

Final points

The dress code varies in Italy depending on what level in the hierarchy you are talking to. At a minimum, you should be professionally dressed. If you want to make a *very good impression* (una bella figura) then you will need to dress stylishly. As in many Latin-Mediterranean countries, you begin by first selling yourself. This happens not through talking about yourself but through the impression you make to the eyes. The higher up the management ladder you go, the more expensive your suit and shoes should be. If speaking to young engineers with no real management responsibilities, it is sufficient to dress smart-casual.

In most cases, Italians will not have the same grasp of the English language as the Northern Europeans do. As a consequence, the language should be made as clear and easy to understand as possible. Native English speakers should learn to use "International English", free of local slang, idiomatic expressions and strong regional accents.

Finally, don't be bothered if members of your audience take a call on their cell phones during your presentation which would require them to leave. Italians must always be accessible to their superiors. Always! Responding to their superiors will trump any requirement to attend a presentation. Just carry on... and be flexible.

III. Dos and Don'ts

With regard to presentations the Italians need or like:
- That your company has a history and good reputation
- A professional speaker who is knowledgeable and cultured
- Only a loose structure
- A flow to your talk that gives the impression of being talked to
- A well-developed background
- Meaningful digressions that hook back into the central theme
- Concrete examples
- Repetition of important ideas
- Well-engineered products with tasteful design
- Solutions adapted to their situation
- Ideas tied together at the conclusion
- Lively Q&A (which includes comments and discussion)

...and they don't need or like:

- Hype or hyping, too much enthusiasm
- Criticism of anyone directly
- Details for their own sake
- Too much theorizing in business presentations
- Rigid structure with no room for flexibility in your talk

10

Making Presentations
in Japan

I. Presentation Profile - Japan

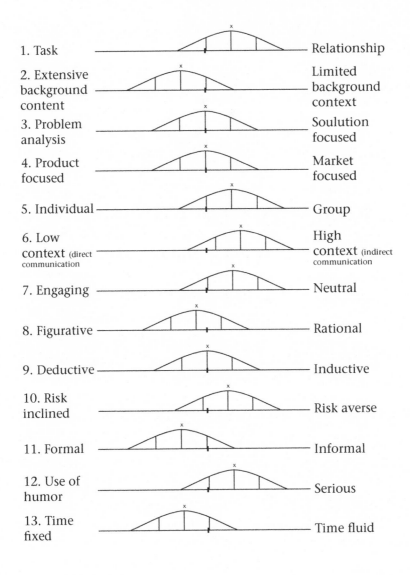

1. Task   Relationship

2. Extensive background content   Limited background context

3. Problem analysis   Soulution focused

4. Product focused   Market focused

5. Individual   Group

6. Low context (direct communication   High context (indirect communication

7. Engaging   Neutral

8. Figurative   Rational

9. Deductive   Inductive

10. Risk inclined   Risk averse

11. Formal   Informal

12. Use of humor   Serious

13. Time fixed   Time fluid

II. Exposé –
Making Presentations in Japan

First things first

Proper protocol is very important to the Japanese - more so than with other Asian cultures. This needs to be kept in mind at all times. It all begins with an exchange of business cards. Present your card with both hands (printed on one side in Japanese which faces up - and the other in English) and accept your counterpart's card with both hands as well, then study it carefully.

In Japan, developing a good business relationship with your contacts is paramount and comes before business concerns. Like the Chinese, but only more so, the Japanese watch and listen carefully to determine who they have in front of them. Things that impress will be your ability to listen, to not talk too much and be silent, to reflect on what you hear, to show interest in others – and to not talk too much about yourself. In the West, "finding out about someone" requires certain facts or explicit information and often comes across like an interview. In Japan, however, one learns about another's *character* by observing how they interact with others. Individuals need to demonstrate harmony (with excellent diplomatic skills), modesty, presence, and "proper" social skills with regard to others. You must be careful of what you express in public (*tatemae*) even if it is not what you personally think (*honne*). For those who feel uncomfortable with such discrepancies, it is best to simply hold your tongue and remain silent (also a supreme Japanese value).

Japan is considered an ascription-oriented culture. That means status is conferred on such things as kinship, gender, age, your connections and your educational background (especially the university you attended). Age is an important "status" and requires that

115

you show demonstrable respect to those who are older. So, the more important the presentation, the more one should consider having an older member of your team deliver it.

The Presentation

The speaker

Do not attempt to make a presentation in the Japanese language unless you speak it *perfectly*. You will need a translator who will also act as a filter for you. It would be best if *you* found a translator who knows something about your company, products and services, etc. When you speak (with a translator) you will need to use an easy English, spoken clearly and *softly*, not too fast, and free of any slang. Even if listeners in your Japanese audience nod their heads to indicate they understand, the chances are they probably don't. Your presentation or proposal, which will also need to be provided in written form (as handouts), will be studied beforehand. Nevertheless, it is important to go through the right steps (the protocol) of making a presentation anyway. In Japan, correct process is more important than end results. You should see the presentation as part of the correct process.

Your body language should be very reserved with minimal gestures and facial expressions. Not only should the voice be softly-spoken, but also the body. In addition, you should avoid looking at your audience members in the eyes. Keep in mind that gazing intensely in someone's eyes is considered a hostile act in Asia.

The tone and manner of the speaker is an important consideration among the Japanese. They very often feel uncomfortable listening to those whose pitch is too high, sound is too nasal, volume is too loud, or manner is too excited. It's best, therefore, to speak in a mid to low pitch of your voice range, soften your volume, and remain as composed as possible.

The opening structure

It is best not to begin straight away with the topic of your presentation. Your Japanese audience will first want to hear about your relationship to Japan, what you've seen in their country, what you liked, why you are there, and how you came to know about their company. Of course, they like to be flattered (not individually, but as a group) and you should do your best to accommodate them. Show that you know about their company, their company's history, products and services – and the respect you have for them.

They will also want to know about *your* company, the department within the company you work for, and even something about your team which they consider highly relevant. It is important that you do not rush through this critical introduction phase. Fifteen or twenty minutes to introduce yourself in this way is not considered long in Japan. In addition, do not underestimate the power of a good reputation to the Japanese. If your company is well-known and has a good reputation, then leverage this fact. The age of a company is important, but a great reputation can be even more important. It will strongly influence how they see your product.

After the non-topic-related introduction, move into the presentation by clearly telling the audience what the main purpose of your talk will be. The purpose statement should be clear and formulated in a way that does not mention what you want to do with the audience (e.g. "I would like to show *you*", "I would like to prove to *you*", "I would like to discuss the advantages/benefits for *you*..."). This could put the audience in an uncomfortable position should the speaker fail to achieve his goals. Rather, it is better to formulate the goal of the talk in a more neutral way (e.g. "I would like to go over *one* possible way to reduce exhaust emissions by 14 per cent"). This formulation allows for the possibility that there may be other approaches to reduce emissions as well.

117

You will then need to explain how you plan to outline your presentation (e.g. usually a slide of main points you will discuss). Your talk should be formal and *structurally well-developed*, with no surprises. Everything you say you will talk about, *should* be talked about (with no additions, deletions or different formulations than what is shown in your outline). The Japanese are quite precise in these matters; they will question (inwardly) your precision if you do not keep to the presentation outline (agenda) exactly as stated. If possible, the outline and most important key points should be handed out in printed form in advance of your talk. It should be well-written and, if possible, with authoritative "quotes" and independent analyses. This is because of the enormous prestige and weight the written word has in Japan.

Like many relationship cultures, the Japanese need to have the background context set for them. In other words, you must precede the main objective (or purpose) of your presentation with a rather extensive "background to the situation". You will need to fill them in with regards to the context. Many Westerners want to "get-to-the-point" as soon as possible, but *miss the point* as to how important building the background context is in Japan. As the Japanese are systemic thinkers, it will be important to demonstrate that you, too, are capable of thinking in terms of relationships – of how one factor impacts another. They want to see these relationships. They also want to see that *you* see them. Therefore, this cannot be a hasty exercise. Be patient and paint a complete picture, showing how the pieces fit together. This will be greatly appreciated, as the Japanese are a strongly visual culture.

Content and points of persuasion

With regard to product presentations, it is important to be very detailed about the different aspects of the product. The Japanese want to be informed about what they regard as the "essential information" of every aspect of a product. This includes reasons for why it was developed and designed in that particular way. You should also discuss the market situation (if something similar already exists in Japan) and even how the price was determined – as well as the factors that may impact the price in the future.

Japanese companies also want information that is context specific. They would like to see data that is directly related to consumer attitudes about the product in a specific situation. Be careful of using general concepts or making general statements that are not linked to specific examples. Examples should be relevant to how a typical Japanese consumer would use something.

One should also be careful to avoid hyped (exaggerated) claims or enthusiastic styles of delivery. Present the facts and be objective and dispassionate. Always demonstrate composure and keep your gestures subdued. A Japanese proverb: "Hollow drums make the most noise".

Providing data in diagram form to support your presentation is very important to Japanese audiences. Hard data is needed to describe what happened in the past. But be careful of trying to extrapolate that data to predict the future. The Japanese are usually skeptical about anticipating the future based on past statistics and number crunching. It is better to quote a respected expert's opinion. In addition, if you have a gut feeling (strong intuition) about something that the data does not support, or for which there is no data, they are very interested in hearing what it is. You need simply announce that this is a strong feeling which seems to contradict the data and they will be eager to hear.

When presenting any theory it will be important to add how your theory will work in practice. The Japanese are acutely aware of the difference between the two. Presenters should not try to find some clever explanation to bridge the two, in order to maintain a logical consistency between the theory and the practical. It is enough to simply admit the difference exists. To say something like, *"That was the theory, but here's how it works in concrete reality"*, will raise the level of interest as well as the credibility of the speaker.

Quality of products and services is an important value that nearly all Japanese companies strive toward. They are aware, however, that quality is an on-going process which must be embedded in a company's operational strategy. It is not enough simply to articulate it in your company's mission statement, but they expect it to be demonstrably part of your culture's mind-set. Any company wishing to collaborate with a Japanese enterprise, will need to show, in some detail, how a continuous-improvement program is part of their company policy. It is one of the keys, if not *the key*, to gaining credibility with a Japanese audience.

Japan is a very high-context culture. They do not like the straight-forward, direct style of communication of the Americans or Northern Europeans. The Japanese, like the circle in their flag, prefer to go around a point rather than straight to it. Information, especially when negative, should be given indirectly – inferring there is a problem without actually stating it. For example, if you need to report that a project is not going well, rather than stating this fact explicitly you could say, *"the team does seem to be progressing nicely and will most certainly improve even more in the coming weeks"*. To the Japanese, the message will be clear. Of course, the use of indirection will require some practice for those not used to this style of communication.

The Japanese are very impressed with real-life demonstrations. So bring along the product and let them handle it if you can. However, avoid bringing along a competitor's products. It is considered taboo in Japan to refer or put the competition in a bad light. *Anything* that can make *anyone* lose face is to be avoided.

The Japanese also want to hear of a product's applications and use - as well as its benefits. You must be able to point out your product's unique selling point, what makes it different. The benefits, however, are best highlighted in terms of the group rather than the individual. This cannot be stressed enough. In Japan, "we" comes before "I". For example, the Sony Walkman in the West was marketed for the listening pleasure of the individual. In Japan, the emphasis was to restrict the sound from disturbing others. Therefore, it is best to avoid expressions which stress advantages for *the individual*. Rather, emphasize the group, we, the harmony of the community or society in general. There is one warning here, however, that you should consider. Talking about "we" can only come once you have actually established a business relationship in the form of supplier-buyer or joint-venture partners. During the relationship-development phase, it is best to avoid using "we" and "us" or you'll come across as pushy and presumptuous, as if your partners have already decided to work with you.

Typically, cultures are categorized as either inductive (Americans) or deductive (French) thinkers. As mentioned above, however, the Japanese are best classified as "systemic" thinkers – analyzing how action in one area may impact another. This does not necessarily mean a cause and effect relationship in the strictest sense, but usually takes a broader view. In other words – you must see how actions impact a *broad circle of potential relationships*. A new technology might be analyzed not only in terms of innovation, but also in terms of its impact on the environment, relationships, work practices and processes, other technology, or even Japanese society as a whole.

The summary

In a way similar to the French, the summary should repeat concisely the important strands that then lead to a logical outcome (the picture you've been weaving together from the beginning of your talk is the key point). Presenting your conclusion in a way that the links are clearly seen (e.g. systemically) will be highly regarded among your Japanese audience.

Q&A

In Japan, it is considered impolite to ask questions during a presentation. Therefore, all requests for questions should be made at the end of your talk. As the Japanese are not confrontational or demonstrative in their communication style, you can expect a low-key approach to questions. Do not expect your audience to engage in an intense discussion or to raise an issue which may contradict the speaker. In numerous cases, it may happen that no-one asks any questions at all. This doesn't mean that the audience was not listening or involved. It may mean that members of the audience simply do not wish to create a face-losing situation for either party. For those who find it difficult to get any feedback at all from a Japanese audience, there is an approach that could help. Allow your Japanese audience to form small groups. Have them discuss and then write down anonymously what points they would like to you to *elaborate* on. Then announce that you would like to collect the questions and take a short coffee/tea break. After returning from the break, respond to the questions.

Final points

You should not be disturbed if, in the middle of your presentation, one or more members of the audience suddenly stand up and walk out, with someone else taking their place. Just go on as if nothing has happened. This is simply giving other members of their team a chance to participate. And should you see some audience members napping – don't worry. They are probably just filling seats to give you a bigger audience.

The Japanese language, even to the Japanese themselves, is an imprecise language. Communication often requires repetition of important ideas. The Japanese will expect to hear these ideas expressed a few times at least - in slightly different ways. This will also be of great help to your translator.

It is a common assumption that the Japanese like to see a presentation that they can read. In other words, with text slides. As hinted at the beginning of this exposé, if you are going to present in English with no translator then they will definitely need text-slides, just to follow what you are saying. However, if a translator is present then it is best to provide the text slides *only as handouts* and simply talk to your Japanese audience – providing helpful visuals only where needed. It is also strongly suggested that you go over your presentation with the translator step by step beforehand. Once you've agreed to what will be covered, stick to it. Surprise comments will most likely lead to a face-losing situation for everyone involved.

For your presentation you should dress conservatively; a dark suit and tie is considered appropriate.

III. Dos and Don'ts

With regard to presentations the Japanese need or like:
- Attention to protocol and established procedures
- Hearing about your company (and its good reputation)
- Seeing that you know their company
- Low-key, polite delivery
- A clear outline – with no surprises
- A well-developed background context
- Systemic thinking/insights
- Context specific applications
- Quotes from recognized experts
- Knowing what is unique about your product or service
- Linking the main threads of your presentation in the summary to form a key message

...and they don't need or like:

- Loud or brash personalities
- Prolonged eye contact (more than a half second)
- Humor
- Emphasis on the individual
- Being pushed for a decision

11

Making Presentations
in Mexico

I. Presentation Profile - Mexico

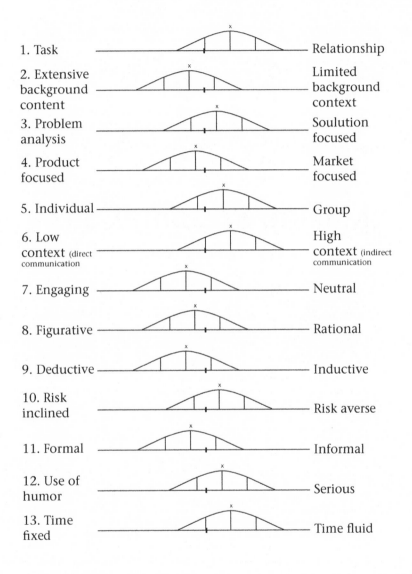

1. Task — Relationship

2. Extensive background content — Limited background context

3. Problem analysis — Soulution focused

4. Product focused — Market focused

5. Individual — Group

6. Low context (direct communication — High context (indirect communication

7. Engaging — Neutral

8. Figurative — Rational

9. Deductive — Inductive

10. Risk inclined — Risk averse

11. Formal — Informal

12. Use of humor — Serious

13. Time fixed — Time fluid

II. Exposé –
Making Presentations in Mexico

First things first

Mexico is definitely a relationship-oriented culture. A genuine personal relationship needs to be established before business can proceed. At a minimum, you will need to convey the feeling that you truly enjoy your business partner's company. To think that a deal can be struck primarily on the strength of a proposal is to set yourself up for certain disappointment.

Mexicans do not look for just superficial niceties. They need to sense truly that you're authentic in your desire to have a relationship with them – and not simply trying to "push the right buttons" in order to satisfy them. Though their manner can be authentically pleasant, their antenna for insincerity is well-developed. In addition, coming across as knowing more than them in your attitude will only intensify their feeling that North Americans and Europeans do not respect them as they should. One example is their resentment at North Americans calling themselves "Americans" – as if other countries in the western hemisphere were not also Americans. Justified or not, they tend to harbor feelings of "hurt pride" that makes them sensitive to not being treated as equals. It is important, therefore, to not give unjustified cause for offence. In part, this is achieved by respecting the hierarchy, seniority, and the formalities of titles while also avoiding an attitude that you're there to "show them how things are done".

It is very important to keep in mind that the topic of the indigenous Indian peoples is a difficult one in Mexico. The Mexican, Nobel-prize-winning author, Octavio Paz, wrote that "Mexico is a schizophrenic culture". To the outside world, Mexicans say that they are "Mexicans". But at home, Mexicans of European, mostly

Spanish, descent (and even the Mestizos, which are mixed Spanish and Indian) say they are Spanish and *not* Mexican. To them, "Indians" (Inditos), who are often seen disparagingly by the ruling and professional class, are those that "dress like Indians and speak an Indian dialect". Therefore, take care not to ingratiate yourselves to Mexicans on this level and with this topic. It is best, at the beginning, to talk about the beauty of Mexico – and leave the topic of "Mexican identity" for them to work out.

The Presentation

The speaker

How you come across to a Mexican audience is perhaps the single most important factor to consider when making a presentation. Finding the right balance in your delivery approach is central and often requires a personality juggling act. You must appear confident and strong (and dress professionally and smartly) or you will not be taken seriously, but at the same time you need to be gracious and friendly. In addition, Mexicans value highly the uniqueness of an individual. One should always allow a chance for the personality to come out but, at the same time, it can in no way be forced or unnatural.

Mexicans like charisma and charismatic speakers, but you should avoid appearing eccentric. You need to be competent and know what you're talking about, but avoid being pedantic at all costs. You should be serious but not take yourself too seriously where it would give the impression of arrogance or severity. Key attributes for a speaker are: authenticity, uniqueness, competence, warmth, politeness, and charisma. You must show respect for status but not be pompous yourself. In other words, with a Mexican audience, one must walk on a razor's edge.

The opening structure

Begin your presentation (introduction) with a personal anecdote – and something positive - about your visit to Mexico without sounding as if you are trying too hard. If you can, try to tie it into your talk so that it flows nicely from the personal to the topic under discussion. You should also say something about yourself and your company if your audience is not yet fully acquainted with them. It's important to point out here, that your structure should not be explicitly stated; rather, it should be embedded, so that your talk has a clear direction to it but is not interrupted by explicit references to outline (e.g. avoid signalling your talk with statements like, "let's now move on to point number 3a"). The basic stages of an effective presentation in Mexico would cover, but not necessarily label, the following: an introduction, the background context, purpose statement, supporting arguments, analysis, descriptions etc., and logical conclusion (that ties everything together) followed by an elegant ending. All of this should be done as if you were simply talking with your audience. Along the way, meaningful digressions can occur - and are usually expected.

After the introduction, you will need to establish the background context of your talk. In other words, before you can move on to the main focus of your talk you will need to explain the surrounding circumstances connected to your topic. Otherwise, it will be difficult for your audience to follow. They will be constantly asking, "Yes, but how did you get to this point? What happened?" One or two lines is probably not enough. So take the time and create a complete picture. Keep in mind that, for Mexican audiences, it's important to establish what the specific difficulty is that you are facing. It is the implicit problem – made explicit, which many North Americans and Northern Europeans fail to adequately convey. The background should not be rushed. And you should try your best to make it interesting and keep it in a narrative form.

After you have established the context, then move on to the purpose by simply indicating that you would now like to look at possible ways of dealing with whatever challenges are implicit in the background story.

Content and points of persuasion

Presentations in Mexico often take the form of an interesting lecture followed by a discussion and the distribution of notes covering the basic points of the lecture. One should not get too mired in details. Mexican audiences prefer to understand the big picture and general principles of a topic supported by credible personal experience.

Mexican communication patterns seldom express explicit prescriptions of what to do, especially among those considered equals or to superiors. Their manner is more indirect, almost tentative, when suggesting a course of action or making any recommendation in general. Therefore, you will probably want to avoid expressions like "you must" or "you have to". In addition, not only are different aspects of one possible choice examined, but different choices are examined as well. This plays a part in avoiding the perception that you are suggesting too forcefully what your audience should do.

This does not hold, however, for presenting established plans or processes where specific instructions are needed to accomplish something. Mexican education stresses learning ideas and concepts all the way through university. Learning how to apply ideas in practical situations is left to the specific situations found in the working world. The logic here is that every situation will be different, so why try to teach a specific application in the university? Therefore, Mexicans are by nature theorists who enjoy the intellectual pursuit of abstract concepts. They have an extremely well-developed ability to conceptualize and perceive problems in global terms, identifying all the influences and visualizing their ramifications. As stated above, for them to really understand the problem they will need to see the whole picture as well as understand the theoretical foundations of what you're proposing. Practicalities of implementation, however, and problem-solving in everyday business situations are weaker points in their training. This is why Mexican subordinates, especially when starting their careers, need specific instructions of what to do. Those who do possess the *know-how of implementation* are highly regarded in Mexico. This means that your presentation of the concrete steps in any process should be approached carefully and iteratively – even broken up (depending on how many steps there are in the process) into a number of presentations.

Scholarly knowledge is important in Mexico with the educated class. They like quotations expressed at the right moment, but not overdone or used simply to show off. This is considered one aspect of *Machismo* – the ability to distinguish oneself intellectually – which includes knowledge of science *and* philosophy (considered impressive in many Latin America countries). They like flowery, colorful rhetoric, sprinkled with anecdotes. To demonstrate a sense of style in the way you speak and to express imaginative ideas will be greeted with great approval in Mexico. One should never subordinate style to structure. Again, some structure should be built into a presentation, but you must also speak unscripted, in a way that keeps the audience's interest.

Self-deprecating remarks, especially with regard to your professional competence, would most likely be confusing to a Mexican audience. If you are an expert in the topic under discussion then it will probably be mentioned by your host when taking the floor. For you to add something like, *"Well, I'm not sure why they sent me, but I'm here now and I hope I don't disappoint you"* would not go over well and probably lead most of them to stop paying attention altogether. After all, if even *you* aren't sure why you're there, then why should anyone listen? They simply would not pick up on your intention to be modest through humor. Likewise, all questions at the end should be answered with an expert's certainty while avoiding brashness or arrogance. It is a type of "soft confidence" that registers on their radar screens. On the other hand, to say, "I don't know" will diminish your standing in their eyes. In Mexico, it is expected that, if you really don't know an answer, you at least offer an intelligent hypothesis or an approximation.

Like many "face-oriented" cultures in the world, Mexicans are good at avoiding confrontation and loss of face. If you have negative, critical information to present them, then never do so directly. Soften the criticism – or, better, express it indirectly. Even criticism that is cushioned should never be done in front of others (or you will have made an enemy *for life*). And finally, criticism should never appear easy for you to give. One should see the pain on your face as well.

Empirical evidence and other objective facts will be examined by Mexicans with a higher education. How you interpret the facts, however, may create resistance among your listeners. For example, international speakers have often encountered what seems to be a contradictory attitude from Mexican professionals. On the one hand, they are interested in what you have to say and will listen politely. On the other hand, there is often a slight resistance to what is being said based on an attitude of "we know better". The way to overcome this is to communicate that you know their situation thoroughly by actually describing that situation in a way that proves it to them. In addition, try to cite as many "locals" as possible (e.g. "Mr Ramirez has pointed out that the market is still developing"). In other words, employ their views as much as possible.

A common stereotype of Mexicans is that they are a happy and optimistic people. Certainly their warmth, gentleness, social gregariousness and strong attachment to family might lead one to this conclusion. But visitors to Mexico should be aware that there is a sadness running deep in the Mexican character that often leads to pessimism about life. They believe that things can go wrong – sometimes terribly wrong. It is nobody's fault. It is simply fate. "Fate", they believe, has many things in store for us that we cannot foresee - and the sequence of events in God's calendar may not correspond to human schedules and plans. Therefore, one should temper one's optimism with an awareness of this reality. To be taken seriously you must show that you are "realistic". You will need to mention that things might not always go according to plan and offer contingency proposals.

Presenters in Mexico should use excellent visuals, but not use them to hide behind. Remember, Mexicans like to see the individual speaker, the person, and not get bombarded by an endless number of PowerPoint slides. If your presentation can be supported with reports or promotional literature, then this would be considered extremely helpful as well (and subject to scrutiny).

The summary

The summary in Mexican presentations is not usually a recap of your main points. Rather, like many Latin American cultures (and Latin Europe) it is a grand ending. All the different strands in the presentation must come together to create an "Aha, now I see it" effect. The body of the presentation is just the build-up to the finale, which reveals the concluding idea or proposition of everything that preceded it. The audience will be listening closely here; therefore, you should have something important to tie together, otherwise they will feel dissatisfied.

Q&A

In the Q&A session which follows the presentation, speakers are expected to be authorities in their field. Never answer, "I don't know" or you will lose credibility. If you don't know, then you are expected to give an intelligent answer anyway.

Final points

It is important to keep in mind that the normal range of voice pitch for Mexican Spanish-speakers is narrower than it is for a number of other languages (especially English, German, Italian and Arabic). The greater range of pitch and volume that is part of "normal" conversation in these other languages is only present in Mexican-Spanish when one is angry. Consequently, Mexicans may experience speakers of these languages to be intimidating. If that's not your intention, then you might consider adjusting your tone and pitch.

III. Dos and Don'ts

With regard to presentations Mexicans need or like:
- A loosely-embedded structure
- Some background context
- Style and individuality
- Eloquence, colorful rhetoric, charismatic speaker
- General principles
- Soft confidence
- Knowledge of their situation
- Contingencies

...and they don't need or like:

- Direct criticism
- Too many details

- Scripted talks
- Openly admitting to not knowing something

12

Making Presentations
in the Netherlands

I. Presentation Profile – The Netherlands

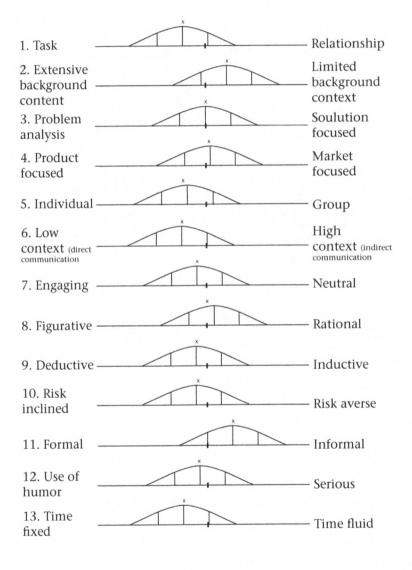

1. Task	Relationship
2. Extensive background content	Limited background context
3. Problem analysis	Soulution focused
4. Product focused	Market focused
5. Individual	Group
6. Low context (direct communication	High context (indirect communication
7. Engaging	Neutral
8. Figurative	Rational
9. Deductive	Inductive
10. Risk inclined	Risk averse
11. Formal	Informal
12. Use of humor	Serious
13. Time fixed	Time fluid

II. Exposé –
Making Presentations in the Netherlands

First things first

The Dutch have a long and successful history as traders. Like many trading countries, they are pragmatic, resourceful, outgoing, and they enjoy a lively exchange of ideas. Combined with the Calvanistic tradition of hard work, modesty, frugality, self-organization, and a strong belief in education as a cornerstone of freedom, one finds a straightforward, democratically-minded, and highly-educated people with a no-frills penchant for business of any size and any kind.

Business will rarely begin a business relationship over any kind of opulent entertainment; a hot drink will be a good start. Weekends are for the family, so don't even bother to think you can squeeze in a Saturday morning meeting. From the Dutch perspective, they claim to make it easy for you to do business with them. They limit the non-essentials to a bare minimum – saving time, money, and energy for everyone involved. One doesn't even need to learn their language – as they are more than willing to speak English at an impressively high level. Therefore, an extensive relationship-building phase is not needed when doing business in the Netherlands. It is a task and achievement-oriented culture that will examine any idea, product or service on its own merits. This does not mean, however, that one should rush quickly into "doing business". They will still want to get to know you and your company first, chatting over coffee. But, after some pleasant and brief formalities, they will be more than ready to "get down to business".

The Netherlands is a strongly egalitarian society. Decisions are made through consensus – often after vigorous debate and consideration. Hierarchies, like the geography of the country, are flat.

Management may be the ones who take a decision, but they must always incorporate the opinions of their subordinates. Interpersonal relationships are informal, with the use of first names usually insisted upon.

Today, Holland (originally Holtland = *woodlands, wooded lands*) is often synonymous with *the Netherlands* in many languages, including English, German, and Italian. This is not formally correct, as Holland is mostly the western coastal region of the country. The Dutch, however, seem to have resigned themselves to this popular inaccuracy about their country. Still, if you refer to their country as the Netherlands, you will win a few points.

The Presentation

The speaker

The Dutch like an unpretentious and knowledgeable speaker. These two qualities cannot be overstated. The speaker should never come across as if he is someone special. They also value learning very highly and, consequently, can be rather demanding as an audience. They expect you to be well-prepared but not read from a script (or from a PowerPoint slide). They do not need to be entertained, but at the same time they do not want a speaker to be stiff and boring (as many Dutchmen and women perceive their eastern neighbor to be when making presentations).

A speaker should also be modest, professional and friendly, yet allow the quality of one's ideas to speak for itself. They disdain exaggeration, self-boasting, and any kind of "hard-sell" approach. You can persuade, but it should be with facts. You can be confident, but not brash. The confidence must be based in *knowing* what you are talking about; you must know your topic area very well, which includes practical experience. Does this mean that a dull speaker has an advantage? Quite the contrary, as a boring speaker (or even a dry personality) will not make a big impression in the Netherlands. A speaker should have some personality and heart (which does not mean charisma) and show that s/he is interested in what they are presenting.

Humor is acceptable when giving a presentation in the Netherlands, though one should not overdo it, or use it when the topic is considered serious.

It is okay to talk about yourself in the introduction, but only very briefly and always in relationship to how you fit into the topic under discussion. One should also avoid being superficial about the Netherlands (e.g. "The tulip fields are beautiful, the windmills are quaint and the canals are picturesque").

The opening structure

The Dutch like a well-structured presentation that gets to the point quickly. The purpose statement should be clear and specific (avoiding generalities); it can also be presented as a question that will be answered with facts and meticulous research. The "question" approach has something to do with the Dutch fondness for formulating an aim in such a way that the listeners will feel they are about to hear something never before heard. Of course, people all over the world like to hear new and interesting things. But the Dutch actually strive to present it, to find that one thing that will make the listener sit up and pay attention.

In the Netherlands, a presentation should always be easy to follow. This is not because the concepts should be easy. Rather, your presentation should have an organized flow to it – in large part through a clear outline that the speaker keeps to. Digressions are rare and hard to follow for a culture used to linear thinking and linear processes. One should add an outline for presentations and make it visible at the beginning of the talk (e.g. the presentation should be divided into four key areas. First... second... etc.). The Dutch also like print handouts which should also be clearly outlined with topic and sub-topic headings, clearly labeled graphs and diagrams and so on. In other words, it should be very well-organized. Sloppiness is looked upon as a reflection of the speaker and company.

Setting the background context should never be too extensive when making presentations in the Netherlands. But it should be included only if needed – and then it should be brief – usually not more than a minute to put your audience in the picture.

Content and points of persuasion

With product presentations, it is important in the Netherlands to present your product or service as objectively as possible. You should focus on the functional virtues of the product or service. You should not only mention its positive sides, but you should also mention some of its negative points as well. This shows strength and will make you look very credible in their eyes. Also, avoid competitive advertising (showing a competitor's product in a bad light). This is disapproved of and seen as hiding some weakness of your own product.

Historically, the Netherlands did not possess natural resources, and the relatively small amount of land they did possess had to be protected against the encroaching sea. To survive, the Dutch learned to rely on their know-how for adding value to local goods or imported raw materials. Therefore, it is important to the Dutch to see what specifically the added value is in anyone's proposal. This needs to be pointed out and should not be left for the audience to assume.

The key to persuading the Dutch is through facts. Emotional appeals, hype, and artificial enthusiasm will backfire badly – even provoking Dutch audiences to openly challenge the speaker. On the other hand, facts that back up your claim will impress. That said, the Dutch are rather cautious even with great ideas supported by convincing data. It is not that they are afraid of risk, but it must be a calculated risk. Therefore, support data should be directed at four broad areas: innovation, added value of a product or service, cost efficiency, and market applicability.

The Dutch tend to score to the right of center between wanting to know about the engineering of a product and wanting to see its potential in the market place. They're interested to know how technology works but not to the degree the Germans and Russians do. They also want to hear *why* a particular feature is important – what specific problem it will solve, or benefit it will add. What are its unique selling points? Speakers who tend to get excited about explaining the intricacies of their technology will need to resist the temptation to go on and on here. Technology should be explained clearly and concisely, but never dominate. If your audience wants to hear more, they will ask. It's more important to show your Dutch audience how to make a profit with what you're proposing.

Related to profit, of course, is the price of a product or service. Usually, the Dutch want to know quite early in the presentation what something will cost (e.g. for manufacturing, wholesale or retail). In many countries, the price would be mentioned at the end after a build-up of its benefits. In the Netherlands, it's the other way round. It is important for them to know at the beginning because they will then listen to the rest of your presentation with the price in mind – constantly comparing (in their heads) if the price-performance ratio is a good one. As one of the most established merchant class cultures in Northern Europe, they know how to buy with exceptional astuteness. One need only compare the price of any products (e.g. automobiles, home appliances, food) between Germany, the UK and the Netherlands (before VAT) and it will almost always be cheaper in the Netherlands. The Dutch are less interested in seeing their product as *luxurious* or of the *highest* quality than they are in getting a good bargain, the best possible deal. They maintain that, *"You should guard every cent you own, fight for every cent you make, and never forget to claim poverty at all times"*. Price, therefore, will be a major factor in winning over your audience in the Netherlands.

One aspect to consider when making a business-related presentation in the Netherlands is the win-win aspect of any proposal. You should be able to demonstrate and explain how specifically both sides will "win". And you should really frame it in just that way. The win-win concept is not so much an *attitude* that the Dutch are looking for in order to clinch a deal; rather, it allows them to see what the speaker is looking for in the proposal as well. They require transparency and will become extremely guarded if a proposal looks too good to be true.

How theoretical can one get on any topic when making a presentation in the Netherlands? Of course, this will depend on your audience and the topic. In general, however, you should consider that the Dutch tend more towards the practical, the pragmatic and the applied than to pure abstraction for its own sake. Theories that are too remote from specific applications do not get them overly excited. They would much rather know what they can do with an idea, how it can benefit someone, or what advantages there are in it. Keep in mind that centuries of fighting back the sea and reclaiming land, dealing with inclement weather, and surviving with no natural resources (apart from North Sea gas and petroleum in the latter half of the 20th century) have given the Dutch a strong pragmatic perspective on life. They admire pragmatic solutions – especially those that can be achieved cost-efficiently.

The Dutch are usually not overly impressed with how detailed your plans are. Rather, they would much more prefer to see that you have thought through the concept you are presenting, that you have considered it carefully. Of course, there should be plans, but they would prefer to see some flexibility built into those plans and processes, knowing very well that unforeseen circumstances are always to be expected. It will be seen as positive, and the speaker seen as practical, if some flexibility is reflected in your plans.

The summary

A presentation summary in the Netherlands should sum up, in one concise sentence (maximum two), the key idea of each topic point that was included in the outline. This should not be a mere review of the headings (e.g. "We looked at the results of the projected sea-level rise over the next 25 years") which, in the end, says nothing. Your Dutch audience will want to hear the idea, or the message that should be extracted from the information you give them. (Many cross-cultural experts have maintained that the Dutch want to hear facts, facts and more facts. While it is true that objective facts can tell their own story, this writer has found that they also want to hear what the speaker's intended interpretation of those facts are, and will attempt even to formulate it for the speaker if it is not included.)

Q&A

Questions from the audience will probably arise spontaneously during the presentation. They will listen critically but objectively. Indeed, the Dutch are some of the most careful and critical listeners in Europe. They will not hesitate to interrupt you and point out a discrepancy in your reasoning or data if they perceive it. They can be very direct and demanding and believe that, by being very honest with you, they are showing you the highest form of respect. So, expect to be called on to defend your claims. Make sure you have your facts at hand. Once your presentation ends, you should still allow for questions and an open discussion at the end.

Final points

It's important to keep to time with the Dutch. If you say your presentation will take only 20 minutes, then make an effort not to run longer than that. The day is tightly scheduled in the Netherlands and nothing can get in the way of leaving work on time to be home with the family. Within the content of the presentation, if you say the delivery of a product or service will take place within a specific period, then stick to it. Even if a delay does not result in a financial loss, the Dutch may demand compensation, or at least a drop in the price.

III. Dos and Don'ts

With regard to presentations the Dutch need or like:
- A knowledgeable, well-prepared speaker
- An interested speaker
- Some humor
- Well-organized and clear structure
- Limited background context
- Learning something new
- Positive and negative sides of a proposal
- Unique selling points – substantiated with facts
- The cost of a product quite early on in the presentation
- The lowest possible price
- The practical, pragmatic and applied over the theoretical
- A concise summary that articulates the key message of each topic
- Your keeping to time
- Time for questions and discussion

...and they don't need or like:

- A dull or uninterested speaker
- Hype or exaggeration
- Too detailed plans
- Digressions

Making Presentations in the Netherlands

13

Making Presentations in Russia

I. Presentation Profile - Russia

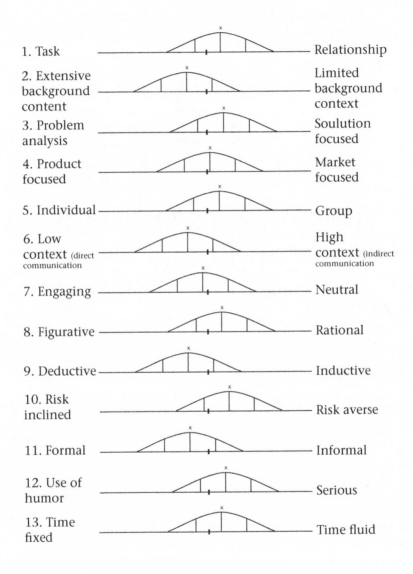

1. Task ——————————————— Relationship

2. Extensive background content ——————————————— Limited background context

3. Problem analysis ——————————————— Soulution focused

4. Product focused ——————————————— Market focused

5. Individual ——————————————— Group

6. Low context (direct communication ——————————————— High context (indirect communication

7. Engaging ——————————————— Neutral

8. Figurative ——————————————— Rational

9. Deductive ——————————————— Inductive

10. Risk inclined ——————————————— Risk averse

11. Formal ——————————————— Informal

12. Use of humor ——————————————— Serious

13. Time fixed ——————————————— Time fluid

II. Exposé –
Making Presentations in Russia

First things first

It is good to prepare your presentation in Russia by first having a good interpreter. They play a very important role when doing business there. Investing time and money in finding an appropriate one will be worth it.

Russian business partners tend to focus on first establishing good relationships rather than on simply making a deal, presenting the facts and getting the task done. Without an established relationship nothing will get accomplished. In Russia, there will always be many random roadblocks to hinder any project up and down the activity stream. And having good relationships and good contacts will act as a lubricant to get things moving. Thus, there is not only a trust factor in the need for relationships, but a strong efficiency one as well. It will take time and require grooming.

Emotion is something Russians like to see in a person, but not straight away. One must build up to it. Russians start off cool and reserved at the beginning of a relationship. They then only gradually warm up when they feel they can trust you (e.g. you seem genuine, show respect, make an authentic attempt to develop the relationship over time, show your human side, can talk easily about non-business matters, know something about Russia, understand the poetic and passionate Russian soul and, of course, drink Vodka).

Russia is a strongly hierarchical culture. All relevant decision-making takes place at the top. So it is best to get those with real authority in the audience if possible.

Finally, it is a good idea to write down your main points and distribute them as handouts to your audience before the presentation begins. If your proposal has to go through bureaucratic channels first, then you will have to present (and translate) your proposal with the background integrated into it as well. Keep in mind, however, that in the final analysis, for Russians, the spoken word trumps the written word – especially in business relationships. It is what you say that is considered binding, not what you write down.

The Presentation

The speaker

In a presentation, begin with a little small talk– but not to sound too smooth or flattering. Don't force it. Be genuine. Russians are extremely mistrustful of foreigners in general. You begin at a deficit. Additionally, do not feel that you need to smile much at the beginning; this will lead them to become suspicious of you. Again, Russians themselves start out with grim faces, but when they do smile it reflects relaxation. This holds true for body language as well. Start off reserved and then gradually increase your expressiveness.

Your delivery should be unhurried – erudite yet sincere. Erudition cannot be overstated here. One thing Russian s very much dislike is an inarticulate speaker. If you are "educated" then you should reflect that education is your ability to speak well. They believe life is complicated, never simple. And your ideas and your ability to express yourself should reflect that. Indeed, the more intricately you can express those ideas, without confusing yourself or your audience, the more you will gain their esteem (another component in gaining their trust).

The opening structure

If you are presenting a proposal, it is good to begin with a general introduction – the background, and history behind the proposal – before proceeding to the particulars. There is no need to rush this phase. Russia is not a protestant culture and, consequently, her people do not feel anxious about time. If you think, "*My audience already knows the background so I can skip over it*" you'll risk wasting a good opportunity to gain the attention and trust of your Russian audience. The audience will want to be assured that *you know* the situation too. Phrase it so it doesn't sound like you're teaching, but confirming a known point. Your understanding of the context will affect their perception of everything that follows in your presentation.

State the purpose of your presentation in clear and specific terms. It does not have to be as concise as typically formulated to native-English speakers or Germans, but it should not be vague or too general either.

Content and Points of Persuasion

For product presentations, it is important to keep in mind that a product per se, good as it may be, is not the most important consideration to Russian business audiences. They will also want to hear about production, the supply chain, service support, marketing and, very importantly, financing (how to get it, how much is needed, who's involved, what conditions, the risks, the costs, etc.).

Russians like to get lots of information. This also goes for technical information related to how a piece of technology was developed; they want to know *how* it works. In part this is because they want to know about all the different aspects of a relevant topic, and partly because they are simply curious; they love to learn. You may need to find a balance between giving them what they want and what they really need. In any case, should you need to explain a process, they will then want a precise description of all the steps involved. If you are describing how a piece of technology works then they will want to know about every facet of it. Information is good, and the more of it the better.

Your Russian audience will also greatly appreciate helpful tools in supporting your explanation (e.g. flipcharts, clear transparencies with diagrams, brilliant analogies, etc.). Text can be put in the handouts but should not be a substitute for visual support that helps make complex ideas easier to grasp.

Russians, on the whole, are a conservative people for whom change is rarely a good thing. Any proposal for change starts off having to overcome a deeply entrenched pessimistic attitude towards it. You will need to explain *why* change is needed and how they will benefit from it.

Russians are quite pessimistic (they say, "cautious") in their view of the world. The world can be dangerous and full of risks, and so can what you are asking them to do in your proposal. If not dangerous then there will be many obstacles in the way. To the Russians, there is no bigger obstacle than the "authorities" and the state bureaucracy, which is always to be mistrusted – and never to be overlooked. Indicating your own distrust of "the system" will win you points. Therefore, be careful of introducing information as an official directive (e.g. EU norms) as if this were a positive point. Likewise, you will lose credibility by promoting any "official" procedure or view of things. In contrast, feel free to present information which stresses a personal perspective, your own opinion, or "unofficially" what you've heard. Russians will be keen to hear it and even consider it more credible.

Further elaborating the points above, Russian business people are always aware of the rules and regulations that are in place, even though they dislike them. Any "pragmatic" solution which does not take into account existing rules and regulations will be greeted with apprehension. That's why Russians need to see that you have at least *considered* the specter of an unfriendly bureaucracy. They are keen to hear how you propose to get around the regulations without getting in trouble. You will gain instant credibility by just acknowledging this problem. (The answer, of course, is to find help in the relationships you've developed – for advice or support or to hook into second-tier relationships that can accelerate or, at times, bypass official channels.)

Russian business, in general, takes a short-term view of most projects. That means, businessmen and investors will be looking for implementation and profits to be in the near term. You can illustrate your activity steps on a timeline if you wish – and this could be helpful. But keep in mind the points we've described above. Unless you have demonstrated that you've understood Russian "complexity" (e.g. the corrupt bureaucracy, the market, the unreliability of suppliers, problems of financing, etc.), your flowchart will appear as a naïve fantasy bordering on the ludicrous. That's why you need to be careful of presenting something as easy, uncomplicated and unproblematic. They will suspect you're hiding something or, more likely, that you have absolutely no idea of their situation.

Feel free to digress from your main point to follow an interesting idea. Russian audiences will not only be able to follow with no problem, but they almost expect that if you are truly competent in the area of your topic then you will be able to explore these related ideas. It is part of giving a complete answer to questions – which they value greatly.

Another aspect of Russian communication patterns is the use of hands and facial expressions to convey ideas and emotions. One should, however, not begin this way but rather be more reserved (but not stiff) at the beginning of a presentation, then gradually use more gestures and express more emotion as your presentation unfolds.

Finally, Russia has become a magnet for investment over the last decade with thousands of North American, European and Japanese enterprises now registered in Moscow. The Russians do not simply want to act as commercial subsidiaries and are increasingly becoming involved in production, distribution and in services. This means that presenting in Russia increasingly means taking into account and explaining to your Russian partners *how they will fit into the bigger picture.*

The summary

It is important not to leave your key message for your Russian audience to arrive at by chance. In Russia, a good presentation will have a clear conclusion with the key message unambiguously stated at the end. Any loose ends must be tied together and their connections should be crystal clear. Russian audiences may have a high tolerance for complexity, but they don't want that complexity to deteriorate into chaos. Complexity for complexity's sake is not their desire. It must finally be tied together in a meaningful outcome.

Q&A

Russians usually do not interrupt a speaker during a presentation. They usually sit quietly and give very few cues to the speaker that they are listening. For some speakers this may be disconcerting, but to Russians it is a sign of respect and courteousness. Therefore, leave ample time at the end of your talk for questions and comments. They will have them – and they will usually be well thought out.

Final points

Keep in mind that public decorum is important in Russia (e.g. one shouldn't wear an overcoat in a public building, lean on walls, have your hands in your pockets when talking with someone, or dress inappropriately according to the circumstances). A presenter should also dress formally and smartly. Some humor is considered okay but not with top managers or powerful dignitaries.

III. Dos and Don'ts

With regard to presentations Russians need or like:
- A tight structure
- A good background context
- A build-up to emotion
- A lot of information
- Technical expertise
- Explanation of "how" things work
- Articulate speakers
- Well-formulated ideas
- Your good grasp of their situation
- The unofficial version, your own opinion
- Going beyond the product
- Meaningful complexity

...and they don't need or like:

- Impersonal delivery
- Change
- Simplistic view of things
- Business over relationships

14

Making Presentations
in Scandinavian Countries

I. Presentation Profile – Scandinavian Countries
(Norway, Sweden and Denmark)

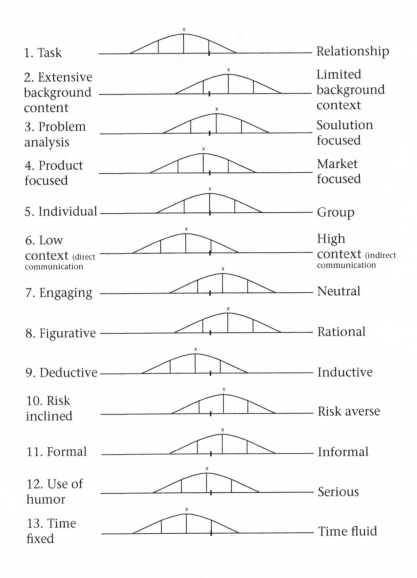

1. Task		Relationship
2. Extensive background content		Limited background context
3. Problem analysis		Soulution focused
4. Product focused		Market focused
5. Individual		Group
6. Low context (direct communication		High context (indirect communication
7. Engaging		Neutral
8. Figurative		Rational
9. Deductive		Inductive
10. Risk inclined		Risk averse
11. Formal		Informal
12. Use of humor		Serious
13. Time fixed		Time fluid

II. Exposé –
Making Presentations in Scandinavia

First things first

No real relationship building phase is needed to do business in Norway, Sweden and Denmark (referred to in this exposé as Scandinavia, or to its people, the Scandinavians). All three countries are achievement-oriented, which means that business dealings are centered around competence, thoroughness and a respect for time. In Scandinavia, business not only comes before relationships, but there's a strong ethos of separation between work and private life in all three countries. Though having a "business" dinner followed by beer drinking afterward is not unusual, you should not expect to be taken care of on weekends should your visit include a Saturday and Sunday.

A common thread that runs through all Scandinavian countries is the deeply-embedded notion of egalitarianism. You should not underestimate the strength of this value in all aspects of communication and behavior, for it can have profound effects on how you're perceived if mishandled. Indeed, in all three countries there is even an unwritten "law" for this concept known as the "law of Jante" (Danish and Norwegian: **Janteloven**; Swedish: **Jantelagen**). There are ten different laws that are defined in Jante. Roughly speaking, however, they can be combined to express the following: *"No matter who you are or what level of success you've reached, never think that you're anyone special or that you're better than us - for even a moment"*. Go against this "law" and you will be viewed suspiciously and, in some case, provoke hostility.

There is a degree of formality running through the Scandinavian cultures. It has to do with respect for one's personal space. For example, you would never ask, "How are you?" unless you really meant it, and then probably with someone who is considered a close friend. It is an attitude that is perceived as Nordic coolness, but really has to do with the high regard for authenticity held by all Scandinavians and the important value of not interfering in someone else's private domain.

The Presentation

The speaker

The Scandinavians usually get down to business right away with just minimal small talk. This attitude reflects how they want to hear and see a presentation. They prefer thoughtful and serious-minded speakers who are authentic and do not *try* to impress in any way. There should be nothing eccentric, though they would like to see something of the person's true personality show through. The speaker should be modest, use clear, unambiguous and unembellished language, and never engage in self-promotion – under any circumstances.

Body language is rather neutral in Scandinavia. Interest and passion are not demonstrated in the expressiveness of the body and facial expressions, but in the content of what you're saying. Excessive body language will probably distract from your message. Scandinavians prefer a low-key approach.

The use of humor will vary among the three countries. In general, the Danes would appreciate some humor during a presentation as well as a slightly more engaging speaker. They, more than their neighbors, like a degree of "hygge" – a feeling of intimate comradeship, even in a presentation setting. This is not the case in Norway and Sweden, where you should be a bit more "reserved" while maintaining a pleasant and polite tone. That said, the Norwegians and Swedes do appreciate people with a good sense of humor – as well as those who exhibit a degree of self-deprecating humor – but they are less disposed than the Danes to use it in the context of business, especially when the topic is serious. For an academic presentation, infusing some humor will usually be well-received

The opening structure

In all three Scandinavian countries you need to structure your presentation tightly. Scandinavians want to hear your main objective (or purpose statement) clearly and concisely. You should be able to articulate it in one sentence or a maximum of two. In Norway and Denmark you will need to give a little background context to your talk. In a way similar to the British, you will need about a minute or two to "put them in the picture". In Sweden, you will need considerably more background. Because more than any other cultural group in Europe, the Swedes come closest to the Japanese in the systemic way they look at the world and the way they solve problems. Therefore, you will need to answer how the current situation got the way it is with all the relevant inputs to that situation included in the picture.

All Scandinavian countries are considered time-fixed cultures. They are conscious of time in the forefront of their lives and expect punctuality in all areas of professional life. It is a good idea, therefore, to list the main points you will be covering as well as announce how long your presentation will take. If you run over the declared time by more than a few minutes, your audience will start to look at their watches.

Content and points of persuasion

In the body of your presentation, all Scandinavians want to "get the facts", but they vary somewhat over the question of amount and emphasis. In Denmark and Norway, it is important to demonstrate the quality of your product with technical information, as well as the quality of your research. Once they are convinced of that, their interest will move to its design, application and marketing potential. You need to convince them with facts, but you should avoid overwhelming them with too much data or they will suspect that you're trying to hide something behind it all. In Sweden, more information is required. You will need to spend more time proving the quality of your product and show how it works technically. Less emphasis should be put on marketing or sales. All Scandinavians will want to know how a product will benefit individual customers, and you will win extra points if you can also demonstrate how society as a whole will benefit.

In all Scandinavian countries, the functionality of a product has been elevated to a very high level. Design is also an important consideration, especially in Denmark. It should be simple, honest, comfortable, sanitary and easy to care for. Their design, commonly referred to as "Nordic Design" and steeped in the democratic tradition, calls for clear and clean lines. These tastes are generally shared across socio-economic levels.

With products and services (or research in academic circles), claims should not be overstated. Be modest and honest. Always tell the truth about a product and do not try to conceal *anything*. Honesty will win you much respect and trust from Scandinavians. On the other hand, if you prove to be dishonest (even slightly), you can pack up and go home.

The Scandinavians appreciate directness and, though they are never ambiguous when they express critique or criticism, they manage to do so in a gentler way than the Germans, Swiss or Dutch. If you need to share something negative, then say it clearly but in an understated tone. Remember to keep the "law of Jante" in mind.

If you have a new version of something, it is acceptable to compare it to the previous version, or even the competition (though you should not name which competitor).

Time references within the content of your talk should be expressed lightly. Any promise you make regarding development time, delivery dates or process steps (especially those that involve your audience) will be taken as fact. Once again, if they prove to be false or in any way exaggerated, then you will be seen as "dishonest", a stigma that will be hard to shake.

All three countries are consensus-driven societies, which will result in time taken to reach a decision. In Sweden and Norway, it may be difficult to even pinpoint who the decision-makers are. You should not insist on knowing who they are, either. Though the Danes are just as egalitarian as their Scandinavian neighbors, they are nevertheless willing to accept a "hierarchy of convenience" within the limited parameters of business. They will not find it offensive if you enquire into who the decision-maker is.

The summary

Summaries are sometimes flat and without the big finish one finds in a typically American presentation. That's because the key information should come during the body of your presentation in Scandinavia. Still, it is a good idea to recapitulate your key point at the end. Your audience will expect it as a type of signal that your presentation is about to finish. A good summary in all three countries requires precision. It does not mean the common practice of simply repeating the outline again (albeit in the past tense). Rather, you should concisely express "the message" one last time. For example, do not say, *"To summarize, we've seen the strategy we should take to remain competitive"*, or *"We've also looked at the significance of what it means for us"*. Rather, precision will require that you say what the strategy *is* and what it *means*. *"To summarize, we've seen that we will need to move into recycled industrial paper if we want to survive in this business"*, or *"We've also seen that moving into this sector will make us much more competitive at little extra cost."*

Q&A

Scandinavians are attentive listeners who will ask questions during your talk when they are unclear about something. It is not considered impolite to interrupt. Speakers should, therefore, be prepared to answer most topic-related questions during the talk and not wait until the end. In all three countries, however, it is not a problem if you don't know a particular fact or can't quote the exact number on something. Your audience will make a distinction between not knowing something specific at the moment (but promising to get back to them on it) and not knowing much at all.

III. Dos and Don'ts

With regard to presentations Scandinavians need or like:
- Modest, authentic and professional speakers with some humor
- Clear structure
- An outline (agenda) of the points you will be covering
- Competence in the subject material
- Quality and functionality of your product
- Clean and clear lines in the design
- Complete honesty about a product
- Unambiguous communication
- Convincing facts
- Your keeping to time
- Simple and clear recapitulation of message at end

...and they don't need or like:

- Self-boasting
- Overstating a claim
- Your thinking you know more than they do

- Your inventing an answer when you're not sure

15

Making Presentations
in South Korea

I. Presentation Profile – South Korea

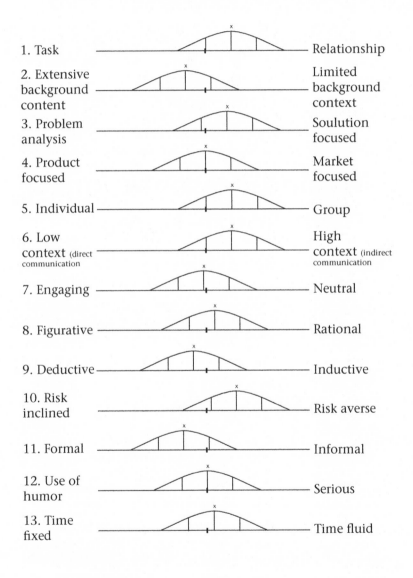

1. Task — Relationship
2. Extensive background content — Limited background context
3. Problem analysis — Soulution focused
4. Product focused — Market focused
5. Individual — Group
6. Low context (direct communication — High context (indirect communication
7. Engaging — Neutral
8. Figurative — Rational
9. Deductive — Inductive
10. Risk inclined — Risk averse
11. Formal — Informal
12. Use of humor — Serious
13. Time fixed — Time fluid

II. Exposé –
Making Presentations in South Korea

First things first

Status is an important value in South Korea. Indeed, Koreans are perhaps the most status-conscious people in all of Asia. If you fail to show the proper respect to a Korean, according to his rank and status, then you will fail before you begin. If you are unsure as to which status someone possesses, then it is best to err on the side of formality. Likewise, sending a speaker with status (age, gender – usually male, and occupying a high position in the company) will lend credibility. If you come from a prestigious university or obtained your degree from one, then this should also be mentioned as it will lift your status in the eyes of your hosts.

Korea is a strong collectivist society that tends to suppress overt expressiveness in their communication style. Connected to this is the concept of *kibun* (similar to "face" in China and Japan), which seeks to maintain a level of well-being (including one's reputation), harmony and correct behavior among its people, even if only on the surface. Much to the exasperation of Westerners, it is very easy to hurt someone's *kibun* by everyday actions such as being argumentative, giving bad news, or ignoring Korean social rankings. Even minor criticisms in any public setting are considered a serious matter. There are unspoken rules which prescribe a level of dignity that must be granted to others, otherwise there is a risk of upsetting one's *kibun*. The one conciliation is that Koreans will make allowances to foreigners (to a point) for protocol mishaps.

On the other hand, though the concept of *kibun* is a more delicate issue in Korea than in other Asian countries, one can, nevertheless, still observe a strong emotional side to Koreans as well.

They try to contain their feelings according to traditional Confucian ideals, but this tends to lead to feelings of suppressed emotions (known as *hahn*) which can, and inevitably do, lead to genuine outbursts.

Korea is considered a drinking culture, especially when developing business relationships. Most business visitors to Korea will be asked if they like "Soju" (a distilled rice wine, similar to schnapps, but tastes like vodka). Your answer should be "yes". For even if you don't like this kind of drink, it will be offered until you agree to try it. You will need to invest energy in the relationship and you will need to invest time. Seeking your own space is not an option.

Learning to develop personal radar (a finely-tuned social antenna) that can pick up on subtle clues is critical for a successful relationship in South Korea. This also means learning to read the context in which messages are communicated. For example, a Korean may say to you, *"Are you hungry?"* (especially around lunch time). In truth, they may actually be saying, *"I am hungry, can we eat now?"* So, if you answer "No" it might put your Korean host in an awkward position. The correct answer would be to ask the Korean what *they* want to eat. This is not an easy skill to learn for most Westerners. But there are a few things you can do to get you moving in the right direction. First, learn to listen more and talk less during personal exchanges. Second, ask relevant questions (but not too many). Finally, make a real effort to reflect before you answer.

You will need to acknowledge that Korea is a unique society, even though they have been influenced and controlled by the Japanese and, to a lesser extent, the Chinese, for centuries before their independence in 1945 (the division into North and South took place in 1948). They are proud and quite defensive of their "own" ways; this should be recognized by visitors as well.

Note: For the remainder of this exposé, South Koreans will be referred to simply as Koreans.

The Presentation

The speaker

The speaker needs to show respect at all times. Your tone should come across as professional but not loud or arrogant. Your speaking volume should be somewhere between the low to middle range. One does not need to be too dry among Koreans as some personality and humor is desirable. But again, don't overdo it. An important consideration, of course, will be who your audience is. If you are giving a presentation below the director level, then you will be permitted to be more informal.

Before beginning with the essence of your presentation, Koreans will first want to know everything about you and your company. As mentioned above, they like status. They want a type of resumé from you: where you studied, what you studied, what your position is within your company, and for what other "well-known" companies you've worked with (as clients). The more "status" you can show, the better. This may seem unnecessary for many, and even cause discomfort to some cultures, but in Korea it is not seen as boasting or immodest. Rather, it is an important factor in establishing trust in one's competence, character, and your company as a potential business partner. They would also like a photograph of you, in the very likely event that your presentation slides are reviewed later or sent to others for review.

A speaker is expected to be well-informed and well-prepared. When questions arise during the Q&A, you will be expected to have your facts on hand to support any claim. Koreans will be less forgiving than many other cultures if they perceive you do not know something pertinent to the presentation topic.

The opening structure

The presentation topic should, of course, be clear to all your listeners. But right from the beginning you should avoid phrasing it in a way that will upset anyone's *kibun*. Avoid formulations that focus on "problem" analysis, on what's wrong with something, or why something won't work. Koreans are usually quite sensitive to a speaker looking at "problems". They're aware that they exist but are confident that they understand them already. So there is no point in focusing your attention here. Besides, focusing on problems might lead the speaker to ascribe - even indirectly – responsibility to an individual or group for the problem. What Koreans want you to concentrate on, most of all, are solutions.

Following a rather concise purpose statement, you will need to present an outline of your talk listing the points you intend to cover. As in other Asian cultures, your outline should contain topic headings that are entirely consistent with those that will appear in the headings later on in your talk. Even minor changes can lead to major confusion and, in some cases, suspicion.

Koreans need a rather extensive background account before moving onto the main body. This is more than just a few lines to "put them in the picture" as typically required in English-speaking countries. Rather, it's a well-developed context that will give them a sense of continuity. It is one that should flow naturally to the main topic of your presentation. The background is also seen as an important element in developing trust in the speaker (and, by extension, your company). If you can show that you understand the various – and, at times, complex - relationships that make up any situation, then you will enhance the audience's perception of competence in you. Keep in mind, however, you will need to walk a fine line here. The speaker will need to demonstrate how different people and elements are all part of a situation (e.g. a given picture) and highlight their association. At the same time, he will need to avoid reducing the analysis to a single cause and effect relationship (just as one line on a canvas does not produce a complete picture).

Like most Asians, Koreans understand that multiple factors make up an event and they will be impressed if they can see that you see this. But, to reduce an explanation of some event to a single "cause and effect" relationship is seen as simplistic and will put the speaker in a bad light. So, be patient and take the time you need to build a picture of how something came to be. Even if the situation is positive, the same principle applies: it cannot be the result of a single cause and effect relationship in the mind of a Korean.

Content and points of persuasion

Koreans are deductive thinkers. They prefer to hear theories and general principles first and then hear appropriate examples that follow from them. Speakers will also win points if they can quote renowned experts in their fields as well as elaborate on their theories.

With regard to products, Koreans tend to be more status conscious than nationalistic in their purchasing decisions (though, in some cases, the two may coincide). What is important is a product's reputation. Again, it need not be a Korean product. Like the Japanese, Koreans will want to hear about product and service benefits couched in the "we" form. One should not highlight how the *individual* gains, but rather how the group benefits.

If, on the other hand, a foreign company would like to set up manufacturing operations in Korea, then Koreans are very much Korea-oriented. You will need to partner with a local company and demonstrate how your product or service will be adapted to local needs.

Persuading Koreans of an idea is no easy task. You can start by showing them specifically the way to profit. At the same time, you will need to keep in mind that Koreans are an exceptionally risk-averse culture. If, in your presentation, you make a proposal that has an 85% chance of succeeding, then your Korean audience will most likely *not* accept it. In Korea, change can be very upsetting, which is why decision-making can take time or simply be put off indefinitely. Persuading Koreans will require many assurances – and guarantees, if possible. It will also require some passion and some emotion on your part, as Koreans must be convinced that the speaker himself is convinced. A warning here, however: your conviction must be sincere as Koreans possess an uncanny ability to discern between genuine and contrived sincerity. Your status and reputation will help, as well as the status and reputation of the other people involved. This is why it is important to refer to your "pedigree" at the beginning of your talk. Again, one major key to success is to find ways to eliminate risk. You may need to suggest a pilot or trial program first before asking Korean decision-makers to commitment on a higher level.

Koreans also like quite a bit of raw data to support your position. But remember, they do not believe much in single cause-and-effect relationships. Therefore, your data will need to be mined from multiple sources and all tied together in an interwoven mosaic that forms an accurate picture of the situation.

To a large degree, Koreans like win-win proposals. Adopting this strategy can help persuade the audience positively, because it demonstrates the credibility of the speaker who is willing to admit he's in it for gain as well. Koreans are, in general, quite suspicious of most foreigners. So revealing your interests will help mitigate that distrust.

South Korean companies can be extremely competitive. So, showing them how they can gain an advantage over their competitors (especially their rivals) will get their attention. Indeed, the pull to gain advantage is so strong that they would prefer relatively short-term advantage benefits to long-term relationships (quite the opposite of the Japanese).

In South Korea, it is considered a valid argument to express a gut feeling about a topic. Koreans like to hear a speaker's own opinion or "intelligent guess" on a situation or potential outcome. Like the Japanese, they still need to see the relevant facts, the numbers, the analysis and support for what you're proposing. But their ears will also perk up when you supply an "off-the-record" honest evaluation of the situation. It is a part of "Nunchi", or a type of sixth sense, that they believe is needed in everyday life.

Among Koreans, there are numerous concentric circles which correspond to the level of familiarity one has with an individual or group. The closer one is to the center, the more one is seen as having an "insider" relationship, with all the benefits and responsibilities that relationship bestows. Specifically, this includes the ability to express yourself on a more candid, explicit level. Conversely, the further away one is the more one is seen as an outsider, and the more indirect and formal your communication style should be. Therefore, indirect communication is especially needed when communicating negative information, which can include technical failures, poor economic results, team conflicts, etc. For example, in a presentation which reviewed the results of the first batch of semi-conductor chips for a European manufacturer in Seoul, the head of quality control needed to inform his Korean team that the chip yields were too low along with other quality concerns. Most Westerners would say something like, *"I'm sorry to report that the yields on our first batch were not what we expected, and that we didn't obtain the quality standards we were aiming for."* This, however, would be considered too direct for most Koreans. A more indirect and acceptable way to communicate this would be, *"Considering that we have a very talented group of engineers on our team, I am convinced that chip yields will only continue to rise."* It would be clear to those present, using this formulation, that there were problems. Lower level managers or team leaders (those "insiders" that are more familiar with the group) would then point out the specific areas that need to be improved. How you say something is almost more important than what you say.

Koreans score left of center along the figurative expression vs. rational expression continuum. As mentioned earlier, they appreciate precise and well-formulated ideas. But they like examples, metaphors and brilliant analogies too. They even like idioms from other languages, as long as they are first prefaced with its meaning (e.g. *"We will need to move quickly on this opportunity – or, as the saying in English goes, the early bird catches the worm"*). It is best to fine tune your language, going for precision rather than bombast, while adding an *occasional* analogy at times (e.g. *"There is growing research that questions whether too much sodium in our diet actually causes high blood pressure, or whether it merely serves as a catalyst for it once it appears"*, or *"This would be analogous to the relationship between wood and fire. Wood does not cause fire, but once a fire has started it becomes an excellent fuel for it"*).

The summary

Summaries for Korean audiences should be given as clear, concise bullet points. They should also build in a coherent sequence that links one idea to the other. The more tightly each summary point idea flows from the previous summary point, the more summary points will be tolerated. *(e.g. 1. International environmental laws are mandating the use of more recycled paper for industrial packaging. 2. In five years, packaging will need to be manufactured from at least 60% recycled paper. 3. Current projections predict a significant shortfall in packaging supply that meets internationally-set standards for packaging content. 4. Retooling to produce recycled paper for the packaging industry will hit a break-even point in only two years. 5. After two years we see a ROI... etc.)* It is important to keep your summary points as objective and neutral as possible. For Koreans, they should be written as plain facts. You should avoid phrasing them in a way that sounds like you are making a pitch or a request for a decision. Your final pitch can be made only after you have first bonded, and it need not be made in a presentation setting.

Q&A

As is typically the case in most Asian countries, Koreans do not generally interrupt a presentation to ask questions. Therefore, you should allow ample time for questions at the end of your talk. One method to ensure questions get asked is to allow your Korean audience to form groups and write their questions anonymously on a sheet of paper, collect them, and then address them after a short break.

Final points

Koreans expect visitors to be on time and follow your presentation agenda scrupulously. However, do not be shocked if your Korean hosts themselves are more flexible with time.

Presentations in Korea are often packed full of data and information. They use PowerPoint as a memo to share information internally. They can even add information to it as it gets passed on.

Dress should be rather conservative, with a suit and tie. On the other hand, avoid over-dressing, even for the top-management level.

Never forget the relationship. Any formal agreements reached are only as good as the quality of your relationship. If the relationship is weak, then any written agreement will probably be worthless.

III. Dos and Don'ts

With regard to presentations the Koreans need or like:
* Respect for hierarchy, status, and the uniqueness of Koreans
* Pedigree from the speaker - and a good reputation

- Well-qualified presenter (with formal titles) in topic area
- A clear outline
- A background context which looks at the separate elements that are associated with a situation
- The facts and the data - as well as an unofficial evaluation of a proposal
- An emphasis on solutions
- The near-term road to profit
- Rational explanations sprinkled with some examples and analogies
- Many assurances and specific suggestions to reduce risk
- Some emotion and passion (must be sincere though)
- Some humor
- Clear, concise and neutral summary points

...and they don't need or like:

- Risky proposals of any kind
- Direct criticism
- An emphasis on problems
- Being pushed for a decision

16

Making Presentations in the UK

I. Presentation Profile - UK

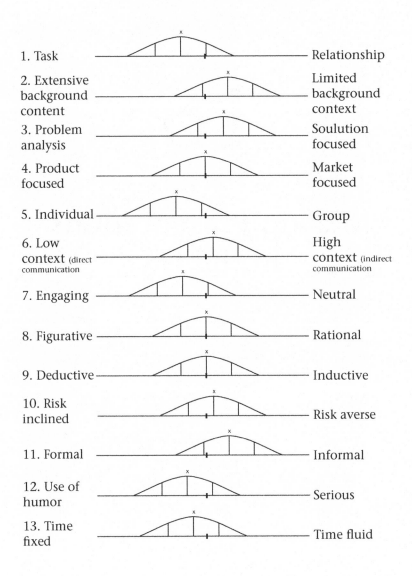

1. Task		Relationship
2. Extensive background content		Limited background context
3. Problem analysis		Soulution focused
4. Product focused		Market focused
5. Individual		Group
6. Low context (direct communication		High context (indirect communication
7. Engaging		Neutral
8. Figurative		Rational
9. Deductive		Inductive
10. Risk inclined		Risk averse
11. Formal		Informal
12. Use of humor		Serious
13. Time fixed		Time fluid

II. Exposé –
Making Presentations in the UK

First things first

Though Northern Ireland is officially part of the UK, references to the UK in this exposé will concentrate only on Great Britain - or the British (those from England, Scotland and Wales).

As in most native English-speaking countries, no real relationship building phase is needed to do business with the British, as one might need in Asia or the Middle East. The British do expect interaction with people (business-related or otherwise) to be friendly, cordial and light at the beginning. Some small talk is required. You should be able to listen politely and refrain from talking too much about yourself. Dress is usually formal (a dark suit) but interactions with each other are rather informal. The British prefer to use first names and do not generally use titles.

The Presentation

The speaker

For presentations in Britain, the speaker should be a competent *speaker*. However, he or she need not always be an expert in the topic under discussion, as the British tend to value generalists over those with narrowly circumscribed knowledge. As long as the topic is interesting and can be presented clearly, then it should be well-received. The speaker should also be natural (e.g. unaffected, without any contrived enthusiasm), modest and honest. If there is an area connected to your topic with which you are not familiar, then it is no problem in Britain to admit it. Indeed, it's better to admit it than to get caught trying to bluff the audience. Your British audience will have no problems with the former but object to the

181

latter. In a similar vein, *taking yourself too seriously (or even appearing to take yourself too seriously)* will be met with considerable disapproval. You risk distracting the listener from your message if this perception is too strong and may even provoke your audience to begin "taking the mickey out of you" (tease you) until you can "lighten up".

The British love humor in all areas of life and presentations are no exception. Using humorous comments and anecdotes throughout a presentation is one way to liven-up a dull topic. And it can often be used to diffuse a tense situation. In addition, humor helps the audience feel comfortable with the speaker. That said, one should be careful of trying to "force" humor. If you don't feel confident in using it, then leave it. You can compensate for the lack of humor by being friendly, open and approachable. Things to avoid include self-promotion and being too absolute in your opinion (an attitude that there is no discussion or other interpretation of the facts other than yours). "Absolutism" is usually unwelcome in most cultures, but it is a particular turn-off in Britain.

In general, the British like to hear a presentation in a narrative form. This can be a story or series of stories that all tie together to make a point; there must be a connecting thread to them. The use of stories is also an effective way to make your message memorable and easy to relate to. But, most importantly, it keeps the presentation (and especially the speaker) from being boring, which would be a crushing evaluation in Britain.

The opening structure

If you are giving a business-related presentation then any account of your company (i.e. history, product line, main market) should be brief. Avoid lengthy company chronicles. In business, the British are more interested in where your company is today and where you're headed in the future.

In most Anglo-Saxon countries, with Britain being no exception, a presentation should be well-structured with a clear beginning, middle and end. You must articulate what your objective is and how you plan to reach it (using an outline for business presentations) at the beginning of the talk. What you should avoid, however, is to over-structure your talk into sub-points and sub-sub points and so on. A British audience wants the presenter to speak freely but within a loosely structured framework, and they prefer a general overview to excessive detail.

You should also provide some background to your talk, though it should be brief – just enough to get your audience "in the picture".

The content and points of persuasion

With regard to your content, the British often want to hear how particular problems will be solved. *"What is going to work?" "What will get us out of this problem?"* The quicker it will solve a concrete problem, the better. Indeed, if it comes down to choosing between listening to someone who can help you out of a problem and someone who will help you "get ahead", the problem-solver will be preferred.

For product presentations, keep in mind that pragmatism is the avenue of persuasion in Britain. Products should look good (nice or classy) but, in the end, the highest consideration will be a product or service's functionality. This should be presented in a straightforward manner without any hype. The information must provide the confidence to act. Some points to consider are the following:

- What it can do
- Production costs
- An acceptable price
- How it can speed up a process especially compared to the current system, service, or product
- The long-term view (especilly if something will need to be changed or altered due to new laws or norms)
- Examples of use/how it performed
- Explain the effects (e.g. reduced waiting time in hospital).

Comparing products or services with the competition is acceptable in Britain. However, you should not be critical of the competitor but let the "facts" speak for themselves (e.g. "The chocolate content of our product is 10% greater than product x [the competitor's]").

For persuasive presentations, you will need to provide enough information (as with products and services) to give the listener the confidence to act. There must be a clear benefit for the individual, group or society. Appealing to emotions should be avoided. Rather, you will need to convince your audience of the "rightness" of what you are proposing by using common-sense arguments. You will also need to present the drawbacks of not doing what you are advocating.

One way to convince and impress your British audience that you have really thought about a solution you are proposing is to be able to present a few options (variations) of that solution. For example, if you are proposing a way "to reduce pollution in the city center", it would be best to go over a number of meaningful alternatives. At the beginning, you should not show a preference for any alternative but simply present them as genuine possibilities – with advantages *and* disadvantages to each. Once you have demonstrated that you have been fair and objective, the audience will then want to hear your personal preference. They will also want to hear the justification for your choice.

The British also appreciate a speaker who can use the English language well. Unlike many other European cultures, the British reserve a special admiration for those who can express themselves eloquently but, at the same time, concisely and with pin-point accuracy. Long, convoluted formulations are the product of an undisciplined mind and may be interpreted as an inability to use the language well or possibly even a device to hide something.

It is rare to give or get direct criticism or specific instructions in Britain. Being too direct will give the impression that you're arrogant and lack tact and social intelligence. For that reason, criticism and instructions should be embedded in diplomatic language. The importance of tact cannot be overstated here.

Finally, you should avoid a hard pitch in Britain. Coming across as overly eager (e.g. trying too hard) will backfire and give the impression that what you are presenting cannot stand on its own merits. You must allow space for your British audience to decide without being pushed or hurried in any way. An exercise in the classic British use of "understatement" may serve you well here.

The summary

British audiences generally don't like to be told explicitly what they should *remember* at the end of a presentation. There's no need to draw special attention to it. If the overall presentation is well-conceived and presented, then it will be clear what the intended message should be. If they agree with it, then that is a different story. You might consider ending your presentation with something to think about. Use softeners such as "I believe" to help avoid sounding too absolute (e.g. *"I believe that, based on what we've heard, we should move swiftly into recycling technology. If we wait much longer, it may just be our company that ends up getting recycled"*).

Q&A

Finally, asking questions during a presentation is acceptable in Britain, so don't be put off if it happens. In most cases, it will only be for clarification. The British believe in fair play and won't ask questions with the intention of trapping you or making you look bad. They will rarely insist on being right, even if they think they are.

III. Dos and Don'ts

With regard to presentations Britons need or like:
- Free speaking within a loose structure
- A narrative quality to your talk
- Humor
- Knowing what is going to solve the problem
- Pragmatic solutions
- An open and approachable speaker
- Specific examples
- Information that provides the confidence to act
- Something to think about at the end

...and they don't need or like:

- Too much structure and detail
- Someone who takes himself too seriously
- Convoluted ideas
- Absolutism in one's opinions
- Direct criticism and instructions

17

Making Presentations
in the USA

I. Presentation Profile - USA

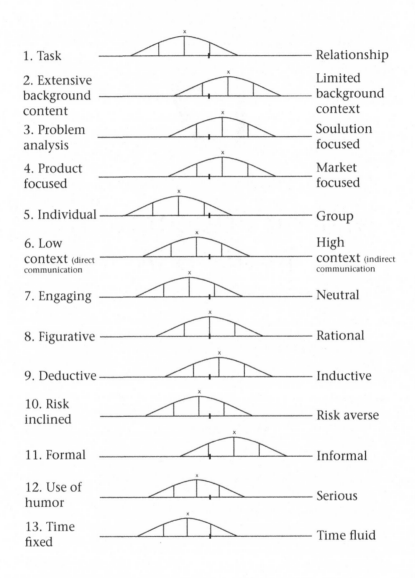

1. Task ——— Relationship

2. Extensive background content ——— Limited background context

3. Problem analysis ——— Soulution focused

4. Product focused ——— Market focused

5. Individual ——— Group

6. Low context (direct communication ——— High context (indirect communication

7. Engaging ——— Neutral

8. Figurative ——— Rational

9. Deductive ——— Inductive

10. Risk inclined ——— Risk averse

11. Formal ——— Informal

12. Use of humor ——— Serious

13. Time fixed ——— Time fluid

II. Exposé –
Making Presentations in the USA

First things first

No real relationship-building phase is needed with Americans. As a task-oriented, achievement-oriented culture they want to see how a product, service or new idea will interest them or their company. The "idea" should speak for itself. They expect the person who will be speaking to be positive, friendly and accessible. One should not be arrogant or come across as overly opinionated. This is the one thing that can quickly sour a potential relationship.

That said, some small talk is in order – usually 5 to 15 minutes, depending on your business partner. Avoid talking about subjects where Americans usually take strong positions (e.g. politics, religion, crime, guns). Small talk to Americans is primarily a chance to "break the ice", to see if you are approachable, open and friendly. They are not looking for personal depth, emotional sincerity, or strong opinions, which Americans will reserve for another context. You will need to have some "antenna" here to ascertain the right time to turn to business. Your American counterpart will usually give you a signal (either saying so explicitly or saying something like, "Well, ah… that's great").

The Presentation

The speaker

Americans like polished, well-prepared, linear-developed presentations where the speaker is interesting as well as interested in the topic being presented. At the same time, it should be informal. Using last names is very uncommon among Americans. Speakers should be friendly, approachable and give the impression that they know what they're talking about. They should appear confident but never arrogant. Humor, and especially a little self-deprecating humor, is usually well-received and an important key in doing business with North Americans in general.

Americans respect those who have a reasonably large vocabulary and can express themselves well. But one should never display it for its own sake. They will react negatively if they think you are trying to "show off" (attract too much attention) by being overly articulate. They have a good nose for people they suspect are speaking down to them.

With an American audience, a speaker should begin by creating a relaxed and amicable atmosphere. This can be done by beginning with a personal anecdote that is connected to the topic. Your self-introduction should include a little about what you do and your professional position (avoid talking about academic titles). Then, you should state the main objective of your presentation clearly and concisely, followed by an outline of the points you'll be covering (see below).

The opening structure

Representing an old, established company is not that important for Americans. If you want to talk about company history, it's okay. But it should be brief. It is more important to talk about where your company is today. Your audience will not be impressed with reputation per se, unless that reputation has been built on consistently well-made products or good service. More important is your latest product or service and the degree to which they can provoke a "wow" reaction (e.g. it's new, it's convenient, and it will surely appeal to the mass market). They want to know how good you are today, and what you can do for them now.

Americans like well-structured presentations. You will need to quickly state your purpose and state it specifically. If they do not know what specifically you are there to tell them, they will become impatient. A detailed background context is rare. It's enough to tell your American audience only as much as it will require to "get them in the picture" (a brief context explanation). They dislike speakers who "ramble on" (speakers who are not concise or talk without a clearly articulated objective).

Americans usually want to hear how you will outline your talk somewhere in the beginning of the presentation. However, you will not need to list the main points of the body if your talk is limited to just one point or follows a clear linear development (e.g. problem and solution).

Content and points of persuasion

For product presentations, a too-detailed, technical explanation should be avoided. General information is enough. If they are interested, *they* will approach *you* afterwards and enquire about details.

Speakers should point out what is special about a product – its unique selling point (Americans may actually use the acronym version: USP). They only care slightly about how something works. They much more prefer to hear what it does, the problems it solves or the need it fulfills. They are results-oriented and want to know how your product, service or idea can help them personally or their company specifically. They like to hear words like "new" and "improved". If there is a new feature, they'll want to hear about it. One thing you should avoid, however, is "overkill". Don't try to list every feature and benefit a product possesses. Americans are content with the one or two that *"make a difference"* – especially from a competitor's version. In the end, you need to make sure your message is easy to remember.

Your arguments should also be persuasive. Americans like to be persuaded – and will give you the chance to do so. It is not enough to present the facts dispassionately; they want to be sold. To do this, you need to appeal to what is pragmatic, practical and demonstrable. And you should avoid talking about features that don't somehow inspire. For example, you cannot say that a product's inner frame is made of a tungsten alloy if it doesn't give them a clear benefit.

Options are important to Americans, even if the differences are not dramatic. And, of course, getting the best price is very positive. In addition, Americans like product comparisons among similarly competitive products on the market. There is no taboo against it, or against naming and comparing your product to a competitor on every level. Indeed, the more prominent the competitor with which your product or service is being compared, the greater impact it will have on the audience.

Americans are usually open to being persuaded on some point. They will invite you to change their minds. But perhaps more than being persuaded, Americans need very much to be inspired. To do that, you will have to show your American audience the "big picture", a compelling vision of where you want to go, of what can be achieved (e.g. *"I see a day, a not too distant day, when smog in Los Angeles will be gone forever"*). So, take some time to develop a picture that is clear and inspiring. You must convey the impression that you know exactly where you're going, even if the details of "how" are not completely worked out yet. Whether it is something as mundane as a new technique for burning fat or something as grand as going to the moon, they will want to hear it in a way that tells them, "this is it", "this is the way", "here's what we need to do" ... and, whatever it is... "it will work". They especially like anecdotes which show how, after numerous challenges, success was achieved.

Americans believe deeply that they have the power to influence their own lives and environment. Not only can things be made better, but "you" personally can take action to make things better, "you" can act to improve your situation. Pessimism is often perceived as surrendering to external circumstances which could be changed if you really wanted to. Numerous other cultures may sometimes criticize Americans for being overly optimistic, based on a superficial understanding of a situation. Americans, on the other hand, see an overly critical, pessimistic attitude as not a weakness of intellect but as a weakness of will. That's why the inspiration factor, in seeking to persuade Americans, should not be underestimated.

American culture, as a whole, values independence. Therefore, any feature of a product or service that can help the individual be more independent (less reliable on others or other circumstances) will be viewed very positively. For example, one of the features of a DVD player that was valued most by Americans in the last decade was its user-friendly, time-delay recording function, allowing consumers to record their favorite TV programs and view them at a more convenient time. Though consumers around the world also appreciated this function, Americans were unique in ranking this feature as high as or higher than the playback picture quality itself.

The striving toward independence is connected to another value of great importance in the United States – that of "time". Time has a material quality to most Americans. It can be saved, lost, wasted, divided, stolen, and monetarily valued – like money. Indeed, *"time is not only money"* (a quintessentially American saying), but it is perhaps the main ingredient in the American love of convenience. There is a strong time-saving element in all things they consider convenient. Therefore, anything that can reduce time in some area means that the individual will gain it somewhere else (allowing for more time to do something else). Where Germans will pay extra for the quality engineering of a product, Americans will pay if your product or service demonstrably saves time (a key benefit in any product presentation).

A second aspect of convenience is connected to the idea of making life easier and more comfortable, which Americans always consider a worthwhile goal. Anything that can reduce what they perceive as *needless physical exertion* is considered not only a benefit but a potentially lucrative money-maker as well. It is probably no coincidence that escalators, electric garage-door openers, power steering in cars, the automatic ice dispenser in refrigerators, and the humble T.V. remote control, to name just a few modern conveniences, were invented by Americans. If your product or service can make life easier, at any level, then expect to get an enthusiastic reception from an audience in the United States.

Americans do not mind some hyperbole – also known as "hype" (the best, the most, the fastest) with an enthusiastic speaker. However, it must *not* be too much. There is a point where even Americans will consider such talk suspicious. They will "smell a rat". They also make a distinction between enthusiasm and emotion. They prefer the former and are suspicious, even uncomfortable, with the latter.

If you make bold claims about something, then you need to be prepared to support those claims. Americans very much like to use clear and simple charts and graphs in presentations to support the positions they make. You will need to cite quantifiable facts and the authority behind them (e.g. the expert, the research institute, the think tank, the journal source, etc. *"Warren Buffet predicts that, in the next two years..."*, *"The Forrester Research Group believes that..."*, *"May I draw your attention to this quote from The Economist..."*). A few good quotes or references to credible research institutes will win points. But, like everything, it shouldn't be overdone.

Slides that are clear, simple, and to the point will also win points. Confusing, irrelevant, or needlessly complex visuals will stir them to impatience. Though more and more people are practicing the bad habit of presenting with text slides, it is enough to provide the text of your talk in written form as handouts – and leave them off your slides. Long sentences or paragraphs will be considered a serious drawback, especially if you are tempted to read them as part of your presentation.

American listeners tend to be inductive thinkers. They like the use of examples and anecdotes in their presentations, and they very much like to hear personal experiences as well. When giving examples, real life examples will work best. Take, for example, a new process that speeds up insurance claims. It's not enough to say, *"Our process consulting can help your company"*, or even *"Our process consulting will speed up claims control in your company"*. Rather, Americans want to hear specifics. They want to hear how long this insurance company was taking to process claims before implementing the new process, how much faster it got, what savings they accrued, if they could leverage the faster service to sell more policies, etc. They love to hear real-case examples.

As mentioned above, time is a very important quality to Americans - especially with regards to how fast something can be produced, delivered, and installed. Time is money. If there is a breakdown, how fast can it be serviced? The faster, the better.

Americans think they are future-oriented - which really translates into *short-term* future (three months to a year). What will happen with this product? How much market share will be captured? How long will it take to achieve the stated goals? You must convince with facts and figures. In general, they like to hear about short-term gains more than long-term payoffs.

Business people in the US can become interested in "relatively" long-term projects, though under three conditions. First, the project must be uncommonly large in scope or scale where the audience can clearly grasp that the venture will simply take time to achieve. Secondly, the big picture needs to be communicated (and inspiring) where the audience sees that the returns, usually in terms of profits, are even greater proportionately to the time and resources invested. And finally, the time span involved should not exceed five years (8-10 years with government projects such as the Moon mission in the 1960s).

If a new product was developed by a young colleague, they will prefer to hear him or her talk about it rather than the department head. On the other hand, they like to openly challenge an expert's claim if they feel there is a reason. But they will usually do so in a way that does not appear aggressive.

Critique or disagreement is expressed cautiously by most Americans. Disagreement is often introduced first by agreement of some kind, something positive. Softeners are important in American English, which allow Americans to critique or disagree without sounding *critical* or *disagreeable*.

Finally, Americans always want to know what action they will need to take. If there's a plan, what action will they need to do? What are the next steps? Who's involved? How long do you expect it to take? These questions have to be answered or they will be left hanging. The action you require needs to be thought out in general terms; it need not be overly detailed in the early stages of your proposal.

The summary

A good summary is important for your American audience. They like only a few, short and memorable ideas (catch phrases) that they can go away with. Indeed, being able to encapsulate your message into a few memorable short sentences will win you much respect – and very probably increase your chances that they will truly consider your proposal or call to action.

Q&A

Americans often like to ask questions during a presentation and, unless your talk is especially short, you should invite them to do so. You should also invite questions at the end as well – just in case there are some members of the audience who wait until the end. Like your presentation, your responses to questions should also be concise as possible.

Final points

The dress code in the USA depends on the industry and audience you will be addressing. Bankers, investors, top-management executives will require formal business attire (i.e. suit with tie). Speaking to engineers may require anything from smart-casual to a polo shirt and jeans. Academics are usually quite casual when presenting to peers (i.e. the classic jeans and cord sports jacket).

Finally, keep in mind that age, gender, position, and academic degree are, for the most part, irrelevant to Americans. Don't take it personally if you're not given the customary recognition of these "status" symbols you might otherwise receive in your own country. In a society that values "doing" above anything else, you are only as good as what you can produce, create, service and develop *today* - no matter who you are.

III. Dos and Don'ts

With regard to presentations Americans need or like:
- Structure
- Your objective articulated clearly at the beginning
- Being persuaded or "sold" on something
- Being inspired
- Humor – to make the atmosphere light
- Seeing that you're open and approachable
- A product with unique selling points
- Things that promote personal independence, time savings and convenience
- Things that make life easier
- Examples and analogies
- Evidence (e.g. graphs and experts) backing important claims
- Only a few (and easy to remember) key benefit points

...and they don't need or like:

- Too much preliminary relationship building
- Someone who takes himself too seriously
- Being told how to market a product
- Excessive formality

18

Making Presentations
to an Internationally
Mixed Audience

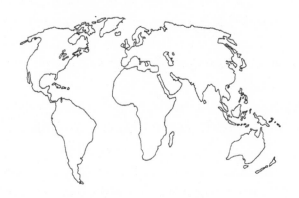

How to Make a Business Presentation to an Internationally Mixed Audience

A parallel question that inevitably arises when writing a book on presenting to specific cultures is what to consider when speaking to an internationally *mixed* audience.

Assuming that the audience is comprised of people with a cross-section of listening preferences, you will probably need to stay close to the middle when using the cultural dimensions for presentations as a guideline. There are, however, three approaches to hug the middle, as well as a number of other factors to take into account, when presenting to a culturally diverse group.

Three approaches

To begin with, in some cases it will require adapting your presentation so that the various styles of *receiving information* are all addressed. For example, include some examples or analogies in your talk even if your preferred style is not to use them. In other words, this is a "little-of-both" approach.

In other cases, especially with *personal delivery* style, a different approach is called for. It involves toning down or intensifying your existing style, especially if it is considered extreme by even your own culture's standard. For a mixed international audience, gestures should be neither too exaggerated nor too restrained. This is a "slight-adjustment" approach.

The third approach entails *enlarging the context to your existing communication repertoire*, essentially stretching a skill into new situations. For instance, most people from low-context cultures are not skilled at being indirect. When they try to be, it comes off as vague and confusing. But they usually do know how to be tactful and diplomatic or hold their opinions in certain situations (e.g. with children or in-laws). The key, then, is to bring that skill into a new context, such as when conveying negative information in a business presentation. Likewise, those from high-context cultures can indeed be quite straightforward when talking to family or friends within their inner circle. They would simply need to apply that skill in a new setting, such as sharing negative opinions more explicitly with the audience. This can be considered a "creative" approach.

To be sure, all these approaches will require some effort and repeated practice before they become a natural part of your presentation skills repertoire.

Other factors to consider

The Language

If the language used for the presentation is English, then it should be "international English", a special imperative for native-speakers. Though there is not yet a consensus as to what a standardized international version of English would be, it is commonly understood that the language should be free of slang, localisms, and most idiomatic expressions. For example, rather than say, *"We will leave no stone unturned in our search for an equitable solution"*, which even proficient non-native speakers would have trouble with, it would be easier for most international audiences if it were rephrased to, *"We will work very hard to find a fair solution"*.

The Speaker

Except for where English is spoken as the native language, most of the world wants to hear a speaker who has solid formal qualifications (even in business) and who is demonstrably competent in the topic under discussion. Speakers should be courteous and professional and avoid coming across in their personal dealings as overly chummy, loud, or ostentatious. Enthusiasm is acceptable, but only if it is rooted in a genuine passion for the topic. Of course, it should never give the impression of being artificial. Dress should also be professional but not overdone. The degree of refinement will also depend on who your audience is (e.g. top or middle managers, engineers, the sales force, etc.).

The Delivery

The range of how different cultural groups would like to experience a speaker, from the soft-spoken, detached, and unaffected delivery of the Japanese to the major swings in volume and emotional intensity preferred in many Arab cultures, is perhaps the broadest of all other categories to be discussed here. As mentioned above, the approach is not to alternate between two extreme styles, but rather to find an approach that is acceptable to all.

Nearly every culture can follow a speaker who is authentic and "talks" with interest and sincerity on almost any topic. It is a "natural" style where the speaker appears almost to be recounting a personal story to the audience. He enunciates clearly, speaks at a medium tempo and pitch, makes eye contact (though not prolonged with Asians), stresses important words or phrases and pauses intermittently to allow the audience to process what was said. This style of speaking, especially with pauses, is of great practical benefit for non-native English-speakers who start off at a disadvantage with the language. It allows them to translate the talk into manageable chunks. It also conforms to a style that is not completely unfamiliar to them.

Structure and Signal Language

Perhaps the most useful support you can give any internationally-mixed audience is to structure your presentation in a way that is easy to follow. One way to do this is to sequence the information in clear steps that are generally understood across cultures. In addition, to make it easier for the audience to know where you are in the structure, it helps to highlight each step along the way by using set phrases, known as signal language (see next page).

The opening structure

1. The self-introduction: If little is known about the speaker, then take a minute to introduce yourself, who you work for and something about your company or department. The length of the introduction will depend on how much time you have for the presentation in total. The subject of the presentation, in most cases, in already known to the audience. If not, you should include this before the self-introduction.

2. Begin the presentation with the background context, which tells the audience about the circumstances that gave rise to the situation you will be addressing. It sets the scene and should be more than a quick comment or pair of sentences. In a mixed cultural setting, one to three minutes should suffice. But most of the world could easily sit through a longer account. For those cultures (Northern Europe and North America) that don't necessarily require a background, the practice of giving one is done by a small percentage of speakers and is growing as a trend; in other words, it is not completely unfamiliar. Therefore, the default setting should be to include one.

3. The purpose statement follows the background context. A frequent question is whether the purpose statement (or objective of the talk) can come *before* the background as well. But if we look at the natural flow of any story, in any culture, we can see that conflict is always introduced first in the story - with attempts to deal with it following afterwards. Likewise,

the purpose statement should articulate how you would like to deal with the situation described in the background. But we must know the situation first.

4. After hearing the situation (the background) and what you want to do about it (the purpose statement), the audience now needs to hear *how* you will go about achieving the goal. Your culturally-mixed audience will find it much easier to follow your presentation if you provide an outline overview of the points you will be covering (e.g. *"I have divided the presentation into three main areas. First, I will offer an analysis of our current market position. Secondly, we will look at... And finally, I am going to cover..."*). In addition, keep in mind that, when you move from one main point to another during the talk, make sure that you repeat the heading as originally stated in the outline overview. Even slight variations can be confusing to those working in a foreign language (e.g. *"Let me now turn to my first point, an analysis of our current market situation."*

The core structure

The core structure (or the body of the presentation) can be highly variable, depending on the topic and purpose of the presentation. It can range from a single talking point that unfolds seamlessly like a story, to a sprawling framework of points, sub-points and sub sub-points. It's probably no surprise that a single, unfolding story is easy to listen to and follow than a presentation with numerous points and sub-points. Of course, sometimes a topic will simply require lots of adjoining points for it to be properly understood. Nevertheless, there is a point where the audience will find it too much to keep up with. To avoid information overload, it is best to follow the rule of three: no more than three main points in the body, and no more than three sub-points for each main point. Bear in mind the closer you can come to the ideal of an unfolding story, the easier it will be for your audience to follow and remember your presentation.

The summary

Over the last 20 years, most summaries have morphed into what I call "pseudo summaries". It is a common practice of simply referring to what the speaker "did" during the presentation rather than what in essence was said (e.g. *"So, I pointed out the strategy we would need to remain competitive in our industry. We've also seen how to... etc."*). This is nothing more than repeating the outline topic-headings in the past tense. Because international audiences already have a difficult time with the nuances of a foreign language, having to concentrate and follow everything during a talk can be a challenge indeed. More than a few audience members confess to feeling tentative about whether they really understood the core ideas of a presentation not in their own language. You can imagine then that a pseudo summary would be of no use for them at all. Therefore, it becomes especially important to help them with a clear, concise, and content-rich summary. *"To sum up, first I pointed out that to remain competitive in the paper industry we will need to move into recycled packaging within 12 months. Second, we have also seen..."*

Q&A

With an international audience, you will need to allow for three levels of Questions & Answers. First, you will have some who will ask questions along the way (e.g. Europeans, North Americans, and Brazilians). Then there are those from cultures who, out of habit or politeness, will only ask questions once the presentation is over (e.g. Asians, Arabs, and Mexicans). Finally, you may find audience members who linger at the end of an official Q&A session and hope to approach the speaker personally. They often have questions that they perceive as indirectly relevant or provocative, or for some reason they thought an earlier answer was not satisfactory.

PART THREE

Using Visual Support

19

A Picture is Worth a Thousand Words

Many business presentations today engage in an audience-un-friendly practice of using slides that are overloaded with text. It's tempting to think that this could be helpful to an international audience. But for the majority of internationally *mixed* audiences whose language skills are usually sufficient enough to follow along, it will be a distraction.

More precisely, we know from our own experience that reading bullet sentences while simultaneously trying to follow what the speaker is saying is a difficult exercise. That's because text projected onto a screen is not really "visual support" per se, even though we've come to think of it as such. Indeed, there's nothing visual about it at all.

Text, at its most basic level, is a symbol (letters, sentences) of another symbol (spoken words) which represents something in our environment. In essence, reading requires the mind to decode symbols at two layers of abstraction with each subsequent layer moving at a slower processing speed. Objects we see (e.g. a tree) travel to our eyes at the speed of light. Spoken language arrives at our ears at the speed of sound, but decoding the sound of the words we hear is a slower process still. And reading is extremely slow in comparison to seeing and hearing. That's why, during a presentation, looking at image-based visuals is effortless, because it moves the audience upward into its fastest cognitive processing mode. Showing text does the opposite. It moves the audience down into its slowest processing mode, which makes it nearly impossible to keep up with the speaker.

It is helpful if the words we read create a fluid mental picture in our head, which is what a story in a novel does. But most business presentations are a collection of fragmented ideas, written as bullet sentences, that the audience has to read while following the presenter at whatever tempo he speaks. Having to read, listen and sometimes look at unrelated pictures (which graphic artists call decorative distractions) can easily overload our cognitive processes. Most of us can't do it. We either listen or read, but not both.

In addition, text slides can be just awful to look at. If we're honest, we would probably have to admit that our own slides are not designed for the listening audience in mind. In most cases we use them as a script for ourselves, reducing the presentation to an absurd exercise in PowerPoint karaoke.

So what can we do to really help our audience? To begin with, we need to tightly structure our presentations in a way that flows nicely and possess a coherent storyline. This alone will eliminate the need for using text on slides. This also means that we need to learn the key points of our own story, and not rely on text slides for our talking notes. This is not to say that good speakers do not use visual support. When they do, however, they are genuinely visual (e.g. diagrams, charts, relevant pictures) and helpful in understanding some idea.

We can also follow two very simple guidelines for designing slides offered by graphic designers. First, we begin by asking ourselves where we will really need them. Where will it be absolutely necessary to help the audience understand a point? Usually, it is needed to make some complex or complicated idea easier for the audience to understand. In other cases, slides can be used to show the audience a compelling example of what you're referring to (e.g. a cut rainforest, a blanket of smog over a city, or a before-and-after comparison). Whatever the content, it will be easier for the audience to process and remember your idea if they can *see* it – and not just read about it.

Next, you will need to ask if you will be able to illustrate the idea effectively or whether you'll need to get help. Visuals should not be too complicated themselves – leaving the audience to scratch their heads and wonder what they're looking at. When looking at a visual, typically a PowerPoint slide, it should quickly provoke an *"Aha, now I understand"* response. If it doesn't fulfill this simple criterion, then there's a good chance the slide(s) needs to be re-designed or even discarded.

Again, text slides are fine as handouts and should be given to an international audience for later reference. But text is a distraction and usually confusing for most audiences if projected on a screen. It will sabotage an otherwise good presentation. In the end, it is best to stick with an old Chinese saying when it comes to using visual support: *a picture is worth a thousand words*. Inverting that formula only leads to confusion and irritation – in everyone's culture.

20

Color, Culture and Visual Support

Certain colors and combination of colors can have special significance in different cultures. A white bridal gown is the symbol of purity in the West, while in India it's the color red. Green is associated with Islam in Saudi Arabia, money in the United States, and a symbol that a man's wife is cheating on him when worn as a green hat in China. The Egyptians associate yellow with mourning, while the Thais connect that emotion to purple. The list could go on.

An important consideration to look at when discussing cultural color associations, however, is the meaning objects and context give to them. On a personal level, if you ask someone to name their favorite color, they usually respond with blue or green or whatever. But when asked if they would want that color to be the color of their teeth or bathtub, they usually decline. It turns out that their favorite color is fine as long as it is restricted to a very narrow list of things or left as an abstract concept.

Likewise, many cultures have learned to associate particular colors to a specific object in a specific context. With other objects of the same color, a different response might be generated, or none at all. A red rose, a red-shaped heart, and a red traffic light may provoke a certain reaction, whereas red poinsettias, a red pocket knife, and a flashing red light atop a fire truck will bring about another.

After more than two decades of holding international presentation seminars, I have not found any significant link between colors used in a PowerPoint presentation and colors that might otherwise convey a special meaning in the speaker's own culture. So, even though white carnations are associated with death in Japan, Japanese business presenters have no problems displaying charts on a white background while wearing a white shirt and occasionally using a white handkerchief to gently pat their slightly perspiring foreheads.

Rather than look at color from a cultural perspective, it may be better to consider it from an optical point of view. We could ask, What will be clearly seen and easy for the eye to distinguish? What colors will provide good contrast and fall comfortably on the retina (e.g. blue, gray, green, crimson, black, etc.)? Your international audience ultimately will want your use of color to be helpful in elucidating your point and to make your ideas immediately comprehensible. They understand that slides used during a business presentation have their own context, which should insulate a speaker against any unintentional misuse of color - and culturally associated meaning.

Appendix One
For International Presentations: the structure and language

Embedded Structure	Signal Phrases (the language of international presentations)
1) **Self-introduction**	Hello L&G, my name is... and I am from... Once again let me introduce myself. My name is... and I represent...
2) **Background information**	As you all know.../ We've all heard of... but what you may not know... *Briefly to put it simply/In a nutshell... The result is/this led to...*
3) **Purpose statement 1** (what the goal of the talk is) **Statement 2** (why the audience should listen)	The purpose of my presentation today is to... What I would like to present to you today is... so that... in order to...
4) **Outline of presentation**	I have divided my presentation into three points/topics... *First/In my first point... I'm going to... Secondly/After this/ We will look at... Third /And finally*
5) **Transition to first point** C	(Now) with regard to my first point... (**REPEAT** 1st Point) Concerning my first topic...
6) **Supporting arguments** (facts, figures, examples, background info) O	I'd like you to look at... /If you look at...*you will notice / as you can see*
7) **Transition to second point**	Turning now to my second point... (**REPEAT** 2nd Point) This brings me to my second point...
8) **Supporting arguments** (facts, figures, examples, background info.) R	As above.
9) **Transition to third point**	And finally, my third point... (**REPEAT** 3rd Point!) Moving to my third and final topic...
10) **Supporting arguments** (facts, figures, examples, background info.)	"

11) **Recommendation** **(optional)** E	At this point I would like to go over some of the options we see open to us. As we see it, there are two possible options. In option one... Now because you mentioned that... *We recommend/we strongly urge...*
12) **Summarizing essential points**	To sum up then. (First we saw, then... and finally **/in 1 -2 sentences**) To summarize my main points.
13) **Thanking and inviting questions**	Thank you for your attention, no doubt you have questions, so.../If you have any questions, please feel free to ask.

Appendix Two
(The Interview Questions)

Below are the questions I used for the interviews relating to my research. Of course, there is a spread to the responses given, as no culture can ever be described at a single point along the value continuums. The question was to identify the critical density of answers that would make this investigation useful. As mentioned in the introduction, I did not rely heavily on what my seminar participants did when giving a presentation. What participants are able to do, and what they recognize as being ideal presentations in their culture, often vary. Culture determines our reference points to a large degree. It provides us with the rules of the game, so to speak; it does not necessarily make us experts at playing that game.

The questions were designed to be used in an interview, as a springboard to dialogue, and not as a questionnaire to be filled in on one's own. This allowed for further refinement of questions – especially with initial responses such as "It depends".

Finally, to avoid the awkward use of "he" or "she", "his" or "her" and "him" or "her" when referring to the presenter/speaker during an interview, I used "they", "their", and "them" even though I'm aware that these are third person *plural* pronouns.

Cultural Dimensions and Presentations

I. **Task vs. Relationship**

1. How important is it to learn something about a speaker about whom you know little or nothing (something personal, professional, about their company etc.)?
2. What other specific information would you want to hear?
3. How much time would you consider appropriate for this part before moving to the topic of the presentation?

II. **Extensive background context vs. Limited background context**

1. To what extent should a speaker set the context of their talk? How much background information do you think is necessary?
2. What specific elements do you think need to be included in the background?
3. How much time, in relation to the whole presentation, should be given to the background?

III. **Problem analysis vs. Solution focus**

1. Which of the following parts would you prefer to hear discussed in greater depth:
    a. The problem
    b. The (proposed) solution
    c. Both problem and solution in equal detail.
2. Which of the following do you agree with most:
    a. The reason many solutions are inadequate is because the problem or the causes are never properly understood.

b. Problems, in most cases, can be easily and quickly grasped. The trick is finding an efficient solution that doesn't require a huge amount of resources.

IV. **Product focus vs. Market focus**

1. In developing a product or service, do you think its success on the market will be determined more by its intrinsic quality and innovativeness, or by how well it's marketed?

2. When hearing a presentation about a new feature in, for example, a mobile phone, would you be more interested in knowing how it was developed and how it works, or in learning what benefit it brings users and how to market it to them?

3. You are going to hear a presentation on an interesting new banking service, developed in Australia that has become very popular. Once you have heard what it is, would you also like to hear how they marketed it in their country? (If the answer was "both" then I would often ask the interviewee to assign a ratio, e.g. 60/40, 35/ 65, 50/50, of time spent on each part).

V. **Individual vs. Group orientation**

1. You are going to hear a presentation on an innovative new power generation technology and *smart grid system* (added in 2005). If you could only choose one, would you rather hear about the benefits this technology and system would bring the society as a whole, or for the individual user?

2. Do you think laws should be made more to guarantee individual liberties or social cohesiveness? (if the answer is "both", then what percentage ratio would you assign to each?).

3. What answer (or ratio) do you think most people in your country would give to question 2?

VI. **Direct vs. Indirect communication (High and low-context communication)**

1. The yield with the first batch of semi-conductor chips in a new plant was quite low. How would you best communicate this to all the engineers *in your culture* working in the Fab (semi-conductor fabrication plant)?

   a. I would need to tell them explicitly, but professionally, that the yield was too low, where in the process we have our biggest problems, and that we would need to improve the process to increase yield values.

   b. I would indicate that, considering we have a top-level engineering team, we could expect rapid movement along the learning curve.

VII. **Engaging vs. Neutral delivery (includes body language)**

1. How would you describe appropriate body language, gestures, voice characteristics, and eye contact during a business presentation? Do you think other people within your culture and professional milieu would agree with you?

VIII. **Figurative vs. Rational expressions**

1. If you were to hear a presentation by a business consultant on a cost-effective way of optimizing your department's processes, would prefer to hear an explanation how it might work in your situation or would you need to see how it was accomplished specifically in another company's real-life situation?

2. If someone were to explain a somewhat difficult and abstract concept to you would you prefer:

    a. A clear, rational explanation of this concept?

    b. A clear, rational explanation of this concept with an analogy or real-life example?

3. When listening to a presentation, do you find yourself automatically waiting for an example or analogy to make complex ideas clearer?

4. How often do you use analogies and examples when explaining a concept?

5. When listening to a presentation in your own language, how often are analogies, examples and anecdotes used in general?

6. When listening to a persuasive presentation, do you think it would be more convincing to hear a poignant story or is it enough to use rational, logical arguments?

IX.   Deductive vs. Inductive thinking

1. If you were to hear a presentation about using text slides in a presentation, what approach would be more convincing to you:

    a. To first hear a general theory about how the mind perceives, thinks and processes information, and then link it to the topic under discussion.

    b. To see the results taken from actual studies on using text slides during a presentation.

    c. To have a little of both (if "c" was chosen, then I would ask them to prioritize "a" and "b" using a percentage ratio, e.g. 60/40, 35/ 65).

X.   Risk inclined vs. Risk averse

1. Which of the following would you agree with most:

    a. It is better to take time and plan thoroughly before you try to implement.

    b. It is better to develop a general plan, but nothing too specific, before you try to implement.

    c. It is better not to plan at all. Just start taking steps on a basic idea or project and see what develops out of that.

  2. Which of the following do you agree with most:

    a. With any proposition, I need to hear the details

    b. With any proposition, I need to see the big picture

    c. With any proposition, I need to discern the speaker's real feelings about the matter

(If the answer was some combination of the three, then I would ask the interviewee to prioritize using a percentage ratio).

XI.   Formal vs. Informal

  1. Please describe what characteristics (about the speaker, the speaker's relationship to the audience, their level of expertise in the topic, and even their style of dress) you would like to see in a presentation from someone who is competent in the topic?

  2. What characteristics about the speaker might significantly diminish your positive perception or level of respect for this person?

XII.   Use of humor vs. Seriousness

  1. Which of the following do you agree with most:

    a. I like to be entertained through humor during a presentation as well as be informed.

    b. I like some humor in a presentation, but it shouldn't be overdone.

    c. In a business presentation context, I don't think humor is appropriate.

  2. How do you think most people in your culture, in general, would respond here?

XIII. Time fixed vs. Time fluid

1. Do you expect a presentation to start punctually? How long should a speaker wait before beginning the presentation, even if some audience members are not there yet?

2. Which of the following statements do you agree with most:

    a. If a presentation runs longer than the stated time, even if I am not obliged to be somewhere else, I usually get irritated.

    b. A presentation can run longer than the stated time – if the topic is important to me and my company.

3. How do you think other people from your country, in general, would respond to the above questions?

Additional Questions

XIV. Likes and Dislikes, Dos and Don'ts

1. What do you like most when hearing presentations from _____ (e.g. Germans, Brazilians, or Swedes)?

2. What do you like least when hearing presentations from _____? (For high-context, face-saving cultures question 2 was formulated differently. For example, "When listening to a presentation from Americans, what would you like to hear more of?" "Where could less time be spent?")

3. What do you think a speaker presenting in your country must absolutely do to make a good impression?

4. What do you think a speaker presenting in your country should absolutely avoid doing in order not to make a bad impression?

XV.   **What do speakers typically overlook?**

1. What do speakers typically overlook (e.g. certain topics, the need to first cultivate relationships, the issue of financing, or whatever) that should be included when making a proposal in your country for:
   - An infrastructure project
   - A joint venture
   - A product or service
   - A manufacturing project.

Note to Readers

I welcome any constructive feedback (positive or negative) you may have regarding the contents of this book. If there is anything you disagree with, or think should be added to the existing profiles, then please feel free to share your comments with me at (welcome@ip-academy.de).

For a possible second edition, I would like to include profiles on Spain, Poland, Turkey, Iran, Indonesia, Malaysia, Thailand, the Philippines, Argentina, Chile, and different regions in Sub-Saharan Africa. If any of you would like to participate in an interview regarding presentation styles in any of these countries, please contact me so that I can send you an electronic version of the questionnaire found in Appendix 2. I would also be happy to interview you on the telephone or through Skype if you prefer.

Bibliography

1. Althen, Gary (1988) "American Ways" A Guide for Foreigners in the United States (Yarmouth: Intercultural Press).

2. Asselin, Gilles and Mastron, Ruth (2001) "Au Contraire" Figuring Out The French (Yarmouth: Intercultural Press).

3. Barzini, Luigi (1964) "The Italians" (New York: Touchstone).

4. Brake Terence, Walker Danielle, Walker Thomas (1995) "Doing Business Internationally" The Guide to Cross-Cultural Sucess (New York: Irwin Professional Publishing).

5. Burgoon J.K., Butler D.B., Woodall W.G. (1996) "Nonverbal Communication:" The Unspoken Dialogue (New York: McGraw-Hill).

6. Carol, Ramonde (1987) "Cultural Misunderstandings" (Chicago: University of Chicago Press).

7. Christopher, Robert C. (1984) "The Japanese Mind" (London: Pan Books).

8. Condon, John C. (1984) "With Respect to the Japanese" (Yarmouth: Intercultural Press).

9. Condon, John C. (1997) "Good Neighbors" Communicating with Mexicans (Yarmouth: Intercultural Press).

10. Field, Michael (1995) "Inside the Arab World" (Cambridge: Harvard University Press).

11. Gannon, Martin J. (2001) "Understanding Global Cultures" Metaphorical Jorneys Through 23 Nations (Thousand Oaks: Sage Publications Inc.).

12. Gesteland, Richard R. (1999) "Cross-Cultural Business Behavior" Marketing, Negotiating and Managing Across Cultures (Copenhagen: Copenhagen Business School Press).

13. Graham, John L. and Sano, Yoshihiro (1984) "Smart Bargaining" Doing Business with the Japanese (Cambridge, MA.: Ballinger Publishing Company).

14. Hall, Edward T. and Hall, Mildred Reed (1990) "Understanding Cultural Differences" Germans, French and Americans (Yarmouth: Intercultural Press).

15. Hill, Richard (1994) "EuroManagers & Martians" The Business Culture of Europe's Trading Nations (Brussels: Europublications).

16. Hofstede, Gert (1980) "Culture's Consequences" International Differences in Word-Related Values (London: Sage Publications).

17. Hooker, John (2003) "Working Across Cultures" (Standford: Stanford Business Books).

18. Hu Wenzhong adn Grove, Cornelius L. (1991) "Encountering the Chinese" (Yarmouth: Intercultural Press).

19. Hu Wenzhong adn Grove, Cornelius L. (1991) "Encountering the Chinese" (Yarmouth: Intercultural Press).

20. Johansson Robinowits, Christina and Werner Carr, Lisa (2001) "Modern-Day Vikings" A practical Guide to Interacting with Swedes (Yarmouth: Intercultural Press).

21. Kohls, L. Robert (2001) "Learning to Think Korean" A Guide to Living and Working in Korea (Yarmouth: Intercultural Press).

22. Kras, Eva S. (1995) "Management in Two Cultures" Bridging the Gap Between U.S. and Mexican Managers (Yarmouth: Intercultural Press).

23. Lamson, Melissa (2010) "No Such Thing as Small Talk" 7 Keys to Understanding German Business Culture (Cupertino CA: Happy About).

24. Leppert, Paul (1996) "Doing Business with Taiwan" (Fremont CA: Jain Publishing).

25. Lewis, Richard D. (2000) "When Cultures Collide" Managing Successfully Across Cultures (London: Nicholas Brealey Publishing).

26. Mente, Boye (2005) "Why Mexicans Think & Behave The Way They Do" The Cultural Factors That Created The Character & Personality of the Mexican People (U.S.: Phonix Books).

27. Mole, John (2003) "Mind Your Manners" Managing Business Cultures in the New Global Europe (London: Nicholas Brealey Publishing).

28. Morrison Terri, Conaway Wayne A., Borden George A. (1994) "Kiss, Bow, or Shake Hands" How to do business in sixty countries. (Holbrook MA: Adams Media Corp.).

29. Morrison Terri, Conaway Wayne A., Douress Joseph J. (1997) "Dun & Bradstreet's Guide to Doing Business Around the World" (Englewood Cliffs: Prentice Hall).

30. Ness, Greg (2000) "Germany" Unraveling an Enigma (Yarmouth: Intercultural Press).

31. Novinger, Tracy (2003) "Communicating with Brazilians" When "Yes" Means "No" (Austin: University of Texas Press).

32. Nydell, Margaret K. (1996) "Understanding Arabs" A Guide for Westerners - Revised Edition (Yarmouth: Intercultural Press).

33. Omari, Jehad (2003) "The Arab Way" How to Work More Effectively with Arab Cultures (Oxford: How to Books).

34. Omari, Jehad (2008) "Understanding the Arab Culture" A Practical Cross-Cultural Guide to Working in the Arab World. 2nd ed. (Oxford: How to Books).

35. Page, Joseph A. (1995) "The Brazilians" (New York: Perseus Books).

36. Richmond, Yale (1992) "From Nyet to Da" Understanding the Russians (Yarmouth: Intercultural Press).

37. Shahar, Lucy and Kurz David (1995) "Border Corssings" American Interactions with Israelis (Yarmouth: Intercultural Press).

38. Sorti, Craig (2007) "Speaking of India" Bridging the Commuication Gap When Working with Indians (Boston: Intercultural Press).

39. Stewart, Edward C. and Bennett (1991) "American Cultural Patterns:" A Cross-Cultrual Perspective (Boston: Intercultural Press).

40. Trompenaars, Fons (1993) "Riding the Waves of Culture" Understanding Cultural Diversity in Business (London: The Economist Books).

41. Turner, Charles Hampden and Trompenaars, Fons (1994) "The Seven Cultures of Capitalism" (New York: Doubleday).

42. Vossestein, Jacob (2004) "Dealing with the Dutch" (Amsterdam: Kit Publishing).

43. Wang Mary Margret, (2000) "Turning Bricks into Jade" Critical Incidents for Mutual Understanding among Chinese and American (Yarmouth: Intercultural Press).

44. White, Colin and Boucke, Laurie (1993) "The Undutchables" An Observation of the Netherlands (Montrose CA: White Boucke Publishing).

45. Wolpert, Stanley (2005) "India" (Berkley: University of California Press).

46. Yoshimura, Noboru and Anderson, Philip (1997) "Inside the Kaisha" Demystifying Japanese Business Behavior (Boston: Harvard Business School Press).

Internet Sources

1. Visual Color Symbolism Chart by Culture:
   http://webdesign.about.com/od/colorcharts/l/bl_colorculture.htm

2. Color Meaning by Culture:
   http://www.globalization-group.com/edge/resources/color-meanings-by-culture/

3. Are your slides killing your presentation?
   http://www.ip-academy.de/node/17

About the Author

Ruben Alexander Hernandez is the founder and president of the International Presentation Academy. Born in the USA but based in the south of Germany, he holds presentation and sales presentation seminars for numerous internationally active companies in Europe, North America and Asia. His focus has been on creating simple but effective methods to train others in the skill of making message-consistent, audience-oriented presentations as well as showing them how to adapt their message to the listening expectations of different cultures around the world. He has published educational readers for the Japanese market, resided in Italy, the UK, and Switzerland, and worked in over 20 different countries. A graduate of UCLA, he holds an MA in Education and an MBA from the OUBS in England. You can contact him by going to www.ip-academy.de.

Made in the USA
Coppell, TX
08 June 2021

57076819R00142